Tokens of Possession

The Northern Voyages of Martin Frobisher

Sir Martin Frobisher

Courtesy of the Bodleian Library, Oxford

Tokens of Possession

The Northern Voyages of Martin Frobisher

W. A. Kenyon

RŌM

Royal Ontario Museum
Toronto, Canada

Printed and bound in Canada by the University of Toronto Press on
70 lb. Rolland S.T. 101.

He that takes upon him to write doth captivate
all the faculties and powers both of his mind and
body and must be only intentive to that which he
collecteth, without any expression of joy and
cheerfulness while he is in his work.

Sir Edward Coke, 1644

Contents

List of Illustrations   viii
List of Maps   ix
Preface   xi
Introduction   1
The First Frobisher Voyage—1576   17
The Second Frobisher Voyage—1577   43
The Third Frobisher Voyage—1578   73
"Frobisher IV"—1974   119
Appendix   157
Index   159

List of Illustrations

Sir Martin Frobisher	ii
Ambrose Dudley, Earl of Warwick	9
Queen Elizabeth I	11
The "sea unicorn"	54
Eskimo, by John White	60
Eskimo woman and child, by John White	61
A skirmish with the Eskimo, by John White	65
The Grinnell Glacier from the air	123
The long-liner	127
The camp at Tikkoon Point	131
Aerial photo of Kodlunarn Island	132
Lincoln Bay	136
Kodlunarn Island from the camp	138
The "ship's trench"	139
The "reservoir or mine"	140
Marks of hand-spiking in the "ship's trench"	143
Best's Bulwark	144
The mine near Native Point	145
View to east from Judy Point	146
Frobisher's house on Kodlunarn Island	148
View from Seagull Rock	150
Rocks from Frobisher's mines	158

List of Maps

Michael Lok's map, 1582   12–13
Beare's map of the world   27
"Frobisher's Straits"   39
Beare's map of Frobisher's Straits   85
Borough's map   100
Frobisher Bay   125
Countess of Warwick Sound   129
Hall's map of Kodlunarn Island   133

Preface

This volume grew out of a general interest in the Canadian north and a specific interest in seeing that the 400th anniversary of Martin Frobisher's first voyage to Baffin Island did not pass unnoticed. For it was Martin Frobisher who started the process of exploration in arctic Canada, a process that is still not completed.

Meetings with some key administrative personnel at the Royal Ontario Museum, particularly Dr. W. M. Tovell, Director, Dr. A. D. Tushingham, Chief Archaeologist, and Mrs. Helen Downie, Programme Secretary, finally led to the following plan. First I would visit Countess of Warwick Sound on Baffin Island with a small archaeological crew to see what I could learn of Frobisher's mining activities. Specimens collected from Frobisher's old mines, together with measurements and descriptions, would form the nucleus of an exhibition to be mounted by the Museum early in 1976. Second, I would prepare a new edition of the three voyages of Martin Frobisher following the text of George Best. His book, *A true discourse of the late voyages of discoverie, for the finding of a passage to Cathaia*, was published in London in 1578 and was the only contemporary account of the three voyages written by a member of the expedition itself. Best was Frobisher's lieutenant aboard the *Aid* on the second voyage and captain of the *Anne Frances* on the third voyage. His *True discourse ...* was subsequently published in 1867 by the Hakluyt Society in Series I, Vol. XXXVIII, edited by R. Collinson. Another edition, by Vilhjalmur Stefansson, entitled *The three voyages of Martin Frobisher in search of a passage to Cathay and India by the north-west, A.D. 1576–8. From the original 1578 text of Geo. Best,* was published by The Argonaut Press, Empire House, 175 Piccadilly, London, in 1938. The latter edition is a two-volume work which reprints every known source that bears directly on the Frobisher voyages, as well as a variety of peripheral material.

The data on the Frobisher voyages, then, are remarkably complete and remarkably well edited. But they are not generally available to the reading public. The present work, it is hoped, will correct this situation, making it possible for the non-specialist to share in the excitement and drama of what is, after all, an important episode in our history. In shaping the present narrative, I make no apology for the liberties I have taken with someone else's story. I have treated it with the respect—and even reverence—which I know it deserves; but at the same time I have pared away the more heroic features of Best's formal declamations, leaving what I believe is a smooth as well as an accurate narrative. I have also modernized the spelling throughout. Occasionally, too, I have substituted a modern term for one of Best's descriptive phrases. For example, his "monstrous great islands of ice" has usually been changed to "icebergs", unless there was some reason for retaining the emotional energy with which his adjectives are charged. I have taken similar liberties with many of his words, particularly substantives, with the result that his "septentrionalis" is usually rendered either "northern" or "arctic", depending on the circumstances, and his "equinoctial" becomes either "equator" or "equatorial".

Besides the support of our administrative staff, the Frobisher project has received enthusiastic assistance from a number of my colleagues. Among them I am particularly grateful to Dr. Henry King, Dr. S. B. Lumbers, Mrs. Jean Charing, Mr. K. C. Keeble, and Mr. David Findlay. Maps and illustrations from outside sources are credited individually, and I gratefully acknowledge the courtesy of those who gave permission for their reproduction. Maps and photographs not individually credited are by the Royal Ontario Museum. Field research on Baffin Island was made possible through the courtesy of the N.W.T. Historical Advisory Board, Government of the Northwest Territories, Yellowknife.

From the inception of the Frobisher project I have had the complete cooperation and assistance of my secretary, Miss Peta Daniels, and my laboratory and field technician, Mr. Michael Lee. They have worked with me for a number of years, and it is a pleasure to acknowledge once more their energy, enthusiasm, and unfailing support. I am grateful, too, for the speed and accuracy with which Miss Margaret Coutinho, Stenographer, Office of the Chief Archaeologist, transformed my edited notes into neat piles of typed manuscript.

Introduction

The way is dangerous, the passage doubtful, the
voyage not thoroughly known.

Richard Willes, 1575

Introduction

By the middle of the sixteenth century, the merchants of England were becoming restless. The known world had been expanding rapidly since the pioneering voyages of Columbus, and undreamed-of wealth was flowing back to Europe along the newly established trade routes; but it was flowing back to Spain and Portugal, not to England. Although the British merchants recognized this as a totally unsatisfactory state of affairs, they accepted, by and large, the prior claims of the continental Europeans. For as early as 1481, Pope Sixtus IV had issued a bull giving all of West Africa south of the Canary Islands to Portugal. Then on May 3, 1493, Pope Alexander VI confirmed Spain's exclusive rights to the New World.

While the states and princes of continental Europe tended to accept these papal decisions, neither Henry VIII of England nor his daughter, Elizabeth I, would recognize the right of the popes to apportion the newly discovered lands in such an arbitrary manner. To challenge the authority of the popes by ignoring their decrees, however, was a different matter; for that would lead directly to a clash with Spain, and Spain was in a position to reinforce her theological arguments with a rather formidable array of sea-power. But if Spain and Portugal could not be too openly challenged, they could perhaps be out-manoeuvred by a diplomatic stance that preserved the amenities, and at the same time permitted the merchants to indulge in a bit of very profitable piracy.

A notable instance was the series of voyages carried out by William Hawkins, the father of Sir John Hawkins. Fitting out his own vessel, the 250-ton *Paul of Plymouth*, the elder Hawkins made three long and remarkable voyages to West Africa and Brazil between 1528 and 1530. Technically, he was encroaching on Portuguese territory because of the papal edict of 1481. In this connection, however, matters of conscience, as well as matters of state, could be dealt with by reference to a prevailing sentiment of the age. For it was firmly believed at the time that an explorer was free to occupy any newly discovered land that was not already occupied by some Christian prince. And Portugal had not actually occupied either West Africa or Brazil, but only parts of them. England's position was expressed most forcibly by Richard Eden, a generation after the pioneering exploits of William Hawkins. Eden said, in effect, that the merchants and traders of England refused to have their movements restricted by the arrogance of the Portuguese who, through "the conquering of fortie or fiftie miles here and there, and erecting of certain fortresses, thinke to be Lordes of halfe the world, envying that other(s) should enjoy the commodities, which they themselves cannot wholy possesse". And so the struggle continued.

English expansion overseas began a period of rapid development in 1553. The voyage which inaugurated this process was the Wyndham-Pinteado expedition to Guinea. Organized by a group of London merchants, the expedition consisted of two ships, the *Primrose* and the *Lion*, and a pinnace called the *Moon*. They were manned by a crew of 140 men "of the lustiest sort". The captain of the *Lion* was Thomas Wyndham, leader of the expedition; the captain of the *Primrose* was a Portuguese pilot, experienced in the Guinea trade, named Anthonie Anes Pinteado. On the way south they stopped at Madeira, where they loaded some wine, and then put into the Canaries before proceeding to tropical Africa.

At the Portuguese fortress of La Mina, in what is now Ghana, the vessels loaded 150 lb. of gold before Wyndham ordered the fleet to follow the coast eastward to Benin for a cargo of pepper. The more experienced Pinteado warned Wyndham that they should return home before they were exposed to the dreaded heat of a tropical summer, but his very sound advice was ignored. Wyndham finally persuaded him to proceed by threatening to cut off his ears and nail them to the mast. At the coast of Benin, they collected eighty tons of pepper over the next couple of months, and only scurried homeward when the men were dying—of fever, presumably—at the rate of four or five a day. Wyndham himself died in Africa, while Pinteado, with his ears intact, died on the homeward voyage. Of the 140 men who had set out on the expedition, scarcely forty returned to Plymouth. Among the survivors was a young lad named Martin Frobisher.

At the same time that Wyndham was leading his tragic but very profitable expedition to the Guinea coast, Sir Hugh Willoughby was leading another small fleet of English vessels into the mists of northern

Norway in search of the northeast passage. This fleet, too, had been sent out by the merchants of London and consisted of three sturdy vessels, each equipped with a pinnace, as well as a ship's boat. The vessels were the *Bona Esperanza* of 120 tons, the *Edward Bonaventure* of 160 tons, and the *Bona Confidentia* of 90 tons. North of the Lofoten Islands, the fleet was scattered by a storm. Richard Chancellor, master of the *Edward Bonaventure* and chief pilot for the expedition, continued to Wardhouse in Northern Norway, where the vessels were to meet if they became separated. He waited there for about a week, then decided to continue the exploration by himself. Sailing east by north, he "held on his course towards that unknowen part of the world, and sailed so farre, that hee came at last to the place where hee found no night at all, but a continuall light and brightnesse of the Sunne shining clearly upon the huge and mightie Sea". (Hakluyt, Vol. I, p. 274, 1927 ed.)

Chancellor finally found his way to Kholmogory at the mouth of the Dvina River in the White Sea, then travelled by sled to Moscow, where he established diplomatic relations with the court of Czar Ivan IV. Sir Hugh Willoughby, meanwhile, had wintered his ships near Kegor in Norwegian Lapland. From documents found on board when the vessels were located, we know that the crews survived the first half of the winter but perished of cold and exposure early in the new year.

Before Chancellor's voyage, European trade with Russia was largely in the hands of merchants from the Low Countries and the Hanseatic towns, who held a virtual monopoly of the Baltic route. As a result of the 1553 expedition, however, this monopoly was broken. The new route to the important resources of northern Russia was immediately explored, and a desperately needed market for English woollens was developed.

The importance of finding this new outlet—or "vent", as it was usually called at the time—can hardly be overemphasized. England's prosperity required a constantly expanding market for her manufactured goods, particularly woollens; and linked with this quest for an expanding market (perhaps even underlying it) was the fear of civil disorder at home. Sir Humphrey Gilbert expressed this anxiety with startling clarity when he was discussing the advantages that would accrue through the discovery of new routes to the Orient and the establishment of overseas colonies. "We might inhabite some parte of those Countreys," he said, "and settle there such needie people of our Countrie, which now trouble the common welth, and through want here at home, are inforced to commit outrageous offences, whereby they are dayly consumed with the Gallows." In addition, the expanded trade would "have occasion, to set poore mens children, to learne handie craftes", and thus there would be no occasion "to have our countrey combred with loyterers, vagabonds, and such like idle persons". To make certain that his message was driven home, Gilbert stated that "he is not worthie to live at all, that for feare, or daunger of death, shunneth his countrey service, and his own honour, seeing death is inevitable, and the fame of vertue immortall".

One of the problems that had to be solved before England could consider herself a serious contender in the struggle for overseas trade was the matter of navigation. English pilots could work their way along the coasts of Europe and Africa, but once they were off the continental shelf they were lost. The overseas voyages of the Spaniards and Portuguese were made possible by their knowledge of the new navigation. For the ancient system of following the coastline from headland to headland and feeling your way across the continental shelf with a lead-line was of no assistance whatever in finding your way across the broad expanses of the ocean seas. For that, a pilot needed to understand celestial navigation. He needed to be skilled in the use of the astrolabe and the cross-staff, and to know enough astronomy to work out his latitude by measuring the elevation of the sun or the north star above the horizon. And these were not subjects that could be learned at sea in the same way that seamanship was learned from an experienced master. An illiterate seaman could learn the ways of a ship and, with experience, could come to recognize familiar landmarks under a wide range of light and weather conditions; but the new navigation was a different matter, requiring the ability to read and write and to use mathematical tables, and at least a smattering of navigational astronomy. These can be formidable subjects even today. To sixteenth-century seamen they were a complete mystery.

The English merchants who were interested in developing overseas trade knew that they could do so only if they had someone to train pilots in the new navigation. To that end, they induced Sebastian Cabot to leave his position as Chief Pilot of Spain and return to England in 1548. One of Cabot's pupils, Stephen Borough, was master and navigator of Chancellor's ship, the *Edward Bonaventure*, when it opened the northern route to Russia in 1553–54. Following the success of that initial voyage, the London merchants incorporated themselves on February 26, 1555, as "The Company of Merchants Adventurers of England for the Discovery of Lands, Territories, Isles, Dominions, and Seigniories unknown", commonly called the Muscovy Company. Michael Lok, a London merchant and ship-owner, was elected governor; Sebastian Cabot served as chief pilot till his death in 1557.

Although the energies of the newly formed company were devoted almost entirely to the development of the White Sea trade during the next few years, the venturers never lost sight of their original objective—to find a new route to the Orient. However, they did nothing about it, apparently, apart from the voyage of Stephen Borough, which extended the White Sea route as far east as the Ob River. But they did remind anyone who challenged their monopoly of northern sea routes that the charter of the Muscovy Company granted them the exclusive right to carry out exploration to the northwest, north, and northeast of England; it also granted the company the exclusive right to trade with any countries that it discovered.

So far as we know, the first person to challenge the monopoly of the Muscovy Company was Martin Frobisher, who had first gone to sea some twenty years earlier with the Wyndham-Pinteado expedition to Guinea in 1553. Frobisher was convinced that a passage existed around the north end of the Americas, and that he could locate that passage if he could arrange the necessary financial support. For several years he appears to have been unsuccessful in promoting his idea, but he was finally able to enlist the aid of Ambrose Dudley, Earl of Warwick. In both financial and social circles, Warwick was a formidable person. He was the third son of John, Duke of Northumberland, and the older brother of Robert, Earl of Leicester, the favourite of Queen Elizabeth. Warwick himself served the crown as both Master of Ordnance and Privy Councillor. It was through the efforts of Warwick, presumably, that pressure was brought to bear on the Muscovy Company. They were told either to undertake the search for the northwest passage themselves or to grant a licence to someone else to carry out the search. After a few brief but pointed political exchanges, Frobisher and his partners were granted a licence in February 1575.

Financial arrangements for the proposed expedition were undertaken by Michael Lok, the London merchant and ship-owner, who was still actively involved with the Muscovy Company. But it was not till the following year that enough money had been raised to equip the expedition, and even then the promoters were operating on a deficit.

The financial organization of the first voyage was as follows: Michael Lok, Sir Thomas Gresham, William Bond, and William Burde each subscribed £100; five other subscribers each contributed £50; and another nine men each contributed £25, thus raising a total capital of £875. With this, they built a small bark of no more than thirty tons, the *Gabriel*, and purchased another, even smaller bark, the *Michael*. In the terminology of the age, a bark was a small three-masted vessel that set a course and topsail on both the foremast and the mainmast and a triangular lateen sail on the mizzen. It also carried a small sprit-sail. Because neither of the barks was large enough to carry the pinnace that would be required for inshore exploration, Frobisher tried to sail one across the Atlantic on her own bottom. She was a tiny vessel of no more than ten tons—probably about the same size as Joshua Slocum's *Spray*—and carried a crew of four. West of the Shetland Islands, the fleet was caught in a heavy gale that lasted eight days, and when the weather cleared the pinnace was gone, lost with all hands.

The eventful course of Frobisher's first voyage is described in George Best's narrative in the following chapter. His difficulties did not end with his safe return to England on October 9. For by that time the original capital of £875 had all been spent, and there were outstanding bills which added up to £738.19s.3d. It would appear, then, that the expedition had been a complete failure, for no new route to the Orient had been located, nor had any new markets been found for the burgeoning woollen trade of England. On the credit side, however, was a piece of black rock, which the expedition had brought back as a "token of possession" from the newly discovered lands, and which appeared to contain some heavy mineral. This was sent by Lok to an assayer, or, more accurately, an alchemist. The assayer's report that the rock contained gold in very valuable quantities put the whole matter in a new light, for it now appeared that Frobisher had stumbled upon a region that contained at least one very rich gold mine, and probably many more as well. Plans were immediately made, therefore, to field another expedition.

When the vessels and stores that had been brought back to England were sold to cover the outstanding debt, they brought in £813.19s.3d., leaving a cash balance of £75. So that the original investors would have an opportunity of recouping the losses they had incurred on the first voyage, it was agreed that both the assets and the liabilities of the first voyage should be transferred to the second. And as the financial prospects of the 1577 expedition looked particularly bright, it was decided to organize the venturers in a more formal manner. An application to the crown was favourably received, and on March 17 a

Ambrose Dudley, Earl of Warwick

Courtesy of the Marquess of Bath

charter was granted to "The Adventurers to the Northwest for the Discovery of a Northwest Passage", or "The Company of Cathay". The new organization was a joint-stock company modelled after the Levant and Muscovy companies. At a meeting in London, the stockholders elected Michael Lok governor, and appointed Martin Frobisher to the position of High Admiral of Cathay, as well as of all newly discovered lands and seas. Heading the list of prominent merchants and courtiers who supported the second voyage was Queen Elizabeth herself, who subscribed £1,000. The total number of venturers was forty-one; the total subscription was £4,275.

The events which followed Frobisher's return from his second voyage were in many respects identical with what had happened after his earlier expedition. The company again lacked funds to pay the men's wages and the other outstanding debts and had to levy a special assessment of 20 per cent on the stockholders to raise the required money. The expedition had brought back from Countess of Warwick Island some 200 tons of what they took to be "gold ore". As there were no facilities available for smelting the "ore", the company had to levy an additional assessment for funds to build two smelters, one at Bristol and the other at Dartford. Together, these levies raised an additional £2,135, bringing the total capital investment in the company to £7,285. Against this capital outlay, the company had a couple of ships, a variety of stores, and a quantity of "ore" that was reputed to be very rich in both gold and silver. For the company had had the "ore" assayed once again, and this time the results were truly amazing. One test reported that a ton of "ore" contained precious metals to the value of £67.1s.8d. Another test reported a value of £53.10s.3d. Juggling such figures was an intoxicating game, and the results were spectacular. For example, it was calculated that an expedition capable of bringing back 2,000 tons of the "ore" could be fielded for £20,836.13s.4d. At a mere £30 per ton, that quantity of "ore" would yield a gross return of £60,000 and a net profit of £39,163.6s.8d. In round figures, then, such a venture would yield a net profit of £20 per ton. With such prospects, the stockholders had little difficulty in raising capital for a third venture, one large enough to return a tidy profit on all the capital that had been expended.

Frobisher's 1578 voyage, with a fleet of fifteen ships and a complement of some 400 men, is still the largest arctic expedition that has ever been fielded. It was also one of the most ambitious. Queen Elizabeth, who provided more than half of the funds initially subscribed, also provided a document entitled: "Instructions given to our loving friend

Queen Elizabeth I

Courtesy of the National Portrait Gallery, London

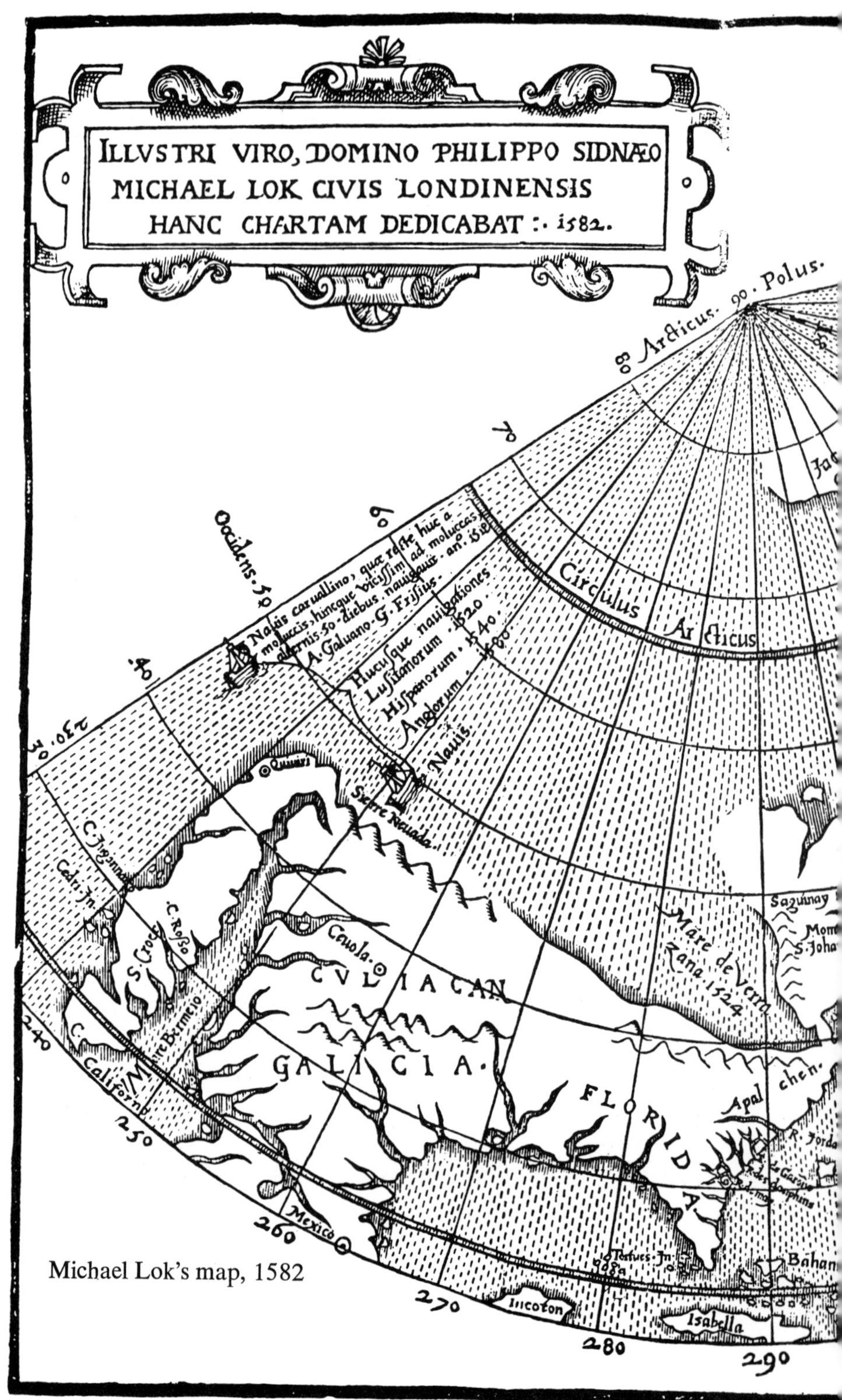

Michael Lok's map, 1582

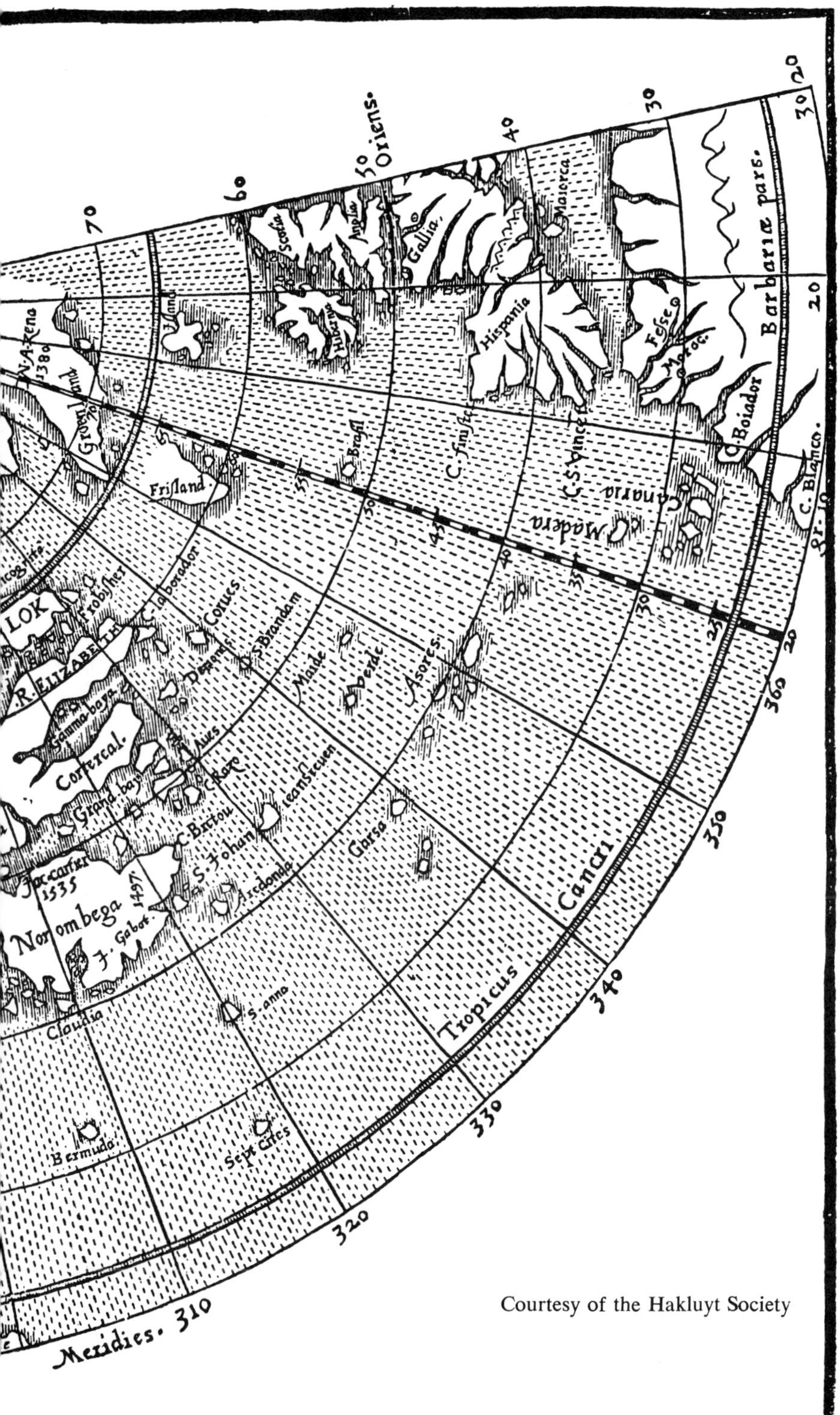

Courtesy of the Hakluyt Society

Martin Frobisher, Esq., for the order to be observed in his voyage now recommended to him for the land now called by Her Majesty Meta Incognita to the northwest parts of Cathay." These instructions, which formally appointed Frobisher to the position of captain general of the fleet, ordered him to set sail before May 1 if at all possible. He was to sail directly to Countess of Warwick Island and there, after looking only to the safety of the vessels and the men, was to start gathering up ore. Only then could he send out parties to search for other, and hopefully richer, mines in the area and to locate a suitable place to erect a settlement. For Frobisher was to leave 100 men in Meta Incognita under the direction of his lieutenant general, Captain Edward Fenton. The wintering party was to consist of thirty soldiers and thirty pioneers, with the other forty made up of seamen, gunners, shipwrights, and carpenters. Three of the vessels—the *Judith*, the *Gabriel*, and the *Michael*—were to be left with the wintering party, together with supplies and food for eighteen months. When the wintering party had been provided for, and when the mining operation was running smoothly, then, and only then, was Frobisher to visit the place where he had lost five of his men during the first voyage, and to explore to the westward. With the two barks, he was to sail 50 or 100 leagues up the strait, or until he was certain that he had passed through the strait and into the South Sea. The general tone of Her Majesty's instructions, as well as many specific details, make it clear that the original aim of the venturers—the discovery of the northwest passage—had been abandoned. Exploration and industrial expansion had both been forgotten. The search, now, was simply for gold, and Frobisher was warned by his sovereign that in all matters pertaining to the mining operation, he "shall cause a record diligently to be kept in writing".

Frobisher's fleet, on this third voyage, dropped anchor in Countess of Warwick Sound on July 30. By August 1 everyone who was not specifically occupied with some other duty was busily digging rock out of the trenches on Countess of Warwick Island. Some of the smaller boats and pinnaces, meanwhile, were scanning the region in search of other places where ore could be dug up and loaded without too much difficulty. Before the short summer ended, the vessels had loaded ore from mines in Beare's Sound and Dyer's Passage, as well as from one mine, called Best's Blessing, on the east side of Queen Elizabeth's Foreland. Along the coast, in the general area of Countess of Warwick Sound, were three particularly rich deposits that were named Countess of Sussex Mine, Fenton's Fortune, and Winter's Furnace. Before they left Meta Incognita for the last time, the vessels had excavated and loaded 1,350 tons of rock. Only 65 tons, incidentally were taken from Countess of Warwick Island. And then, on September 2, 1578, the vessels sailed for home. Frobisher and his officers had wisely decided against establishing a settlement in his "strait", for, as it turned out, the "ore" proved worthless, and they never returned.

*   *   *

Best's ostensible purpose in his *True discourse* was to give an account of Frobisher's three voyages. However, he also had a larger aim in mind. For Best prefaces his account of the three voyages of Martin Frobisher with a learned and tightly reasoned argument on cosmology, an argument that is totally irrelevant today, but only because we have already accepted his main conclusion. We know today that man can live in both the tropics and the arctic; and the curious can very easily learn enough astronomy and geography to cope with the other problems that Best raises. I was tempted, as a result, to delete the entire passage and start the narrative with the departure of Frobisher and his three small ships from England in 1576. But I decided against it, and for the following reason.

Best's *True discourse* is not only a travelogue, although it is, in fact, one of the earliest and finest. It is also an epic, an heroic statement concerning the human condition. Beneath his formal rhetoric we can detect a sense of wonder and excitement at what was happening around him. In retrospect, we shall probably not agree with his evaluation of what was happening in Elizabethan England; but we can agree that those were stirring times. When Frobisher sailed on his first voyage, for example, there were many people still living who remembered the death of Christopher Columbus in 1506. During the intervening years, both the physical and intellectual horizons of man had broadened immeasurably. Best was not exaggerating when he tells us that "it has come to pass that within the memory of man—within these four score years—more new countries and regions have been discovered than in the previous five thousand. In fact, more than half the world has been discovered within the memory of men that are still living."

1576

The First Frobisher Voyage

The worthie Captayne, notwithstanding these dis-
comfortes, continued hys course towardes the
Northweast, knowing that the Sea at length must
needes have an endying, and that some lande shoulde
have a beginning that way.

George Best, 1578

1576

The First Frobisher Voyage

The First Book of the
FIRST VOYAGE OF MARTIN FROBISHER
Esquire, Captain General
for the discovery of the passage to
Cathay and the East Indies by the Northwest,
first attempted in A.D. 1576 on the 15th of May.

Man is not born to look only to his own interests. His friends, relatives, and countrymen also look for some furtherance at his hands and for some of the fruits of his labour. Finding themselves caught up in these bonds and duties of human society, men have tried many ways to show that they were sustaining members of their community. Some of them have sought to devise better laws and ordinances for the government of cities and countries, men such as Solon and Lycurgus. Some have spent their time in devising arts and sciences that would sharpen man's understanding and enable him to express his ideas with greater facility. Thus we have Aristotle for logic and philosophy, Cicero and Demosthenes for rhetoric, and Euclid for arithmetic and geometry. Still others, by long and diligent observation, have charted the courses of the heavenly bodies so that man might distinguish between different times and seasons and thus arrange his activities better, both in work and in play, as occasion and circumstance require. The martial arts delight still others and enable them to defend their country from the threat of the enemy, and rightfully, on occasion, to enlarge their dominions. In a variety of faculties and sciences, men are applying themselves to these matters so vigorously that they deserve to be known as important members of the community. Although these things have happened in the past as well, they are particularly true today. By continual practice and the exercise of sound judgement, the world has now grown finer and more perfect, not only in the speculative arts and sciences, but also in their practical application. The former delight the imagination and show us the nature of things through art and reason; the latter (the mechanical application, which is becoming increasingly common) does so pleasure and profit the world that only this present time may be rightly called the liberal and flourishing age.

For when was there ever such an abundance of gold and silver as in these, our own days? Solomon himself, with all the precious metal of Ophir, had nothing to compare with the vast quantity of gold and other metals which is now being dug out of the bowels of the earth each day and in almost all parts of the world. Lately they have been dug up in lands lying almost under the poles, lands that were formerly supposed to be congealed and frozen. We have grown so wealthy that we are no longer contented with the riches that our ancestors had. We think that we are slothful and lacking in energy if we fail to increase our private wealth and riches in the same proportion as the wealth of the whole world is increasing. And this, not only of gold and silver, but of all things that increase our pleasure and delight our minds, as well as of those things that are necessary for the life of man. For we were placed on this earth to know and acknowledge our Creator and, with gratitude, to take for our maintenance the fruition of things—that is, meat and drink to sustain our bodies, and some covering to defend ourselves against the rigours of heat and cold—and thus to glorify God through our works.

What former age has known such an abundance of necessary meats, or of pleasant and delectable confections, as we know today? We have every kind of corn, grain, and meat that our ancestors had, and have them in far greater abundance; but to this we have added thousands of new things that were never seen or heard of before. The same must be said, also, of things that protect the body. Architecture and building are grown to a new excellence, and cloths and silks of all sorts and colours have become increasingly fine. Man no longer searches for ways to make these things more plentiful, but mainly for ways to make them more fashionable. The cause of this abundance—in addition to divine providence—is the ingenuity of man. Because he is more curious and inquisitive than formerly, he brings out new devices and strange inventions almost daily and causes others to do the same through emulation. Thus he not only provides the necessities that were already mentioned, but keeps up a continual search for new arts, occupations, and faculties.

For example, a device as commodious, necessary, and beneficial as the printing press has lain utterly hidden and unknown until these last few years. And the art of war is now grown to such excellence that if Achilles, Alexander the Great, and Julius Caesar should return, they would stand in admiration and wonder at the courage of our soldiers, their engines, and their policies. They would be even more amazed than were the ignorant and barbarous multitude that celebrated their own achievements. But to draw closer to my own purpose, to discuss inventions that lead to discoveries, I believe that one of the most excellent arts that has ever been devised is the art of navigation. In times past, this was so crude and obscure that no man dared to travel by sea except along the coast. And if wind, current, or tempest were to drive him so far out to sea that he lost sight of land, he made no effort to save himself, for he had but a rude vessel and little skill.

In those days they did not know the singular use and benefit of the lodestone, which is called *magnes* in Latin. Besides the property of drawing iron unto itself, the lodestone points out two principal parts of the earth, the north and the south, and that more distinctly than the rising sun shows east and west, except twice a year at the equinoxes. If anyone would like to see this rare property of the lodestone, let him put the stone in a round dish, and then set the dish in a vessel of water so that it can float freely. When the dish comes to rest, the two principal and opposite points of the stone will firmly and constantly point north and south. If we know which direction is north, and which south, the experiment will show us the two principal points of the stone, for if the one be known the other cannot be wanting. That a man may more surely be persuaded of this effect, let him turn the dish after it has come to rest, and he will find that it always returns to the same point. And if a splinter of steel be but touched with the lodestone and then balanced upon some pyramid or point, it receives such virtue that it acts in the same way. If the splinter of steel is attached to a disc of paper or wood that is divided into thirty-two equal parts, the lines will distinguish and point out all parts of the horizon and will direct the navigator to all the coasts of the world.

This excellent property of the lodestone has been emphasized because many seamen who know this rare and miraculous thing as well as I do, fail to admire it sufficiently, because the knowledge has become so common. Yet the lodestone is to be preferred above all the precious stones of the world, because it serves such a useful purpose, while they have no virtue except decoration. As it is not long since it was first discovered, the use of the lodestone will probably be perfected in this age, and its northeasting and northwesting[1] explained. This is particu-

[1]Compass variation, i.e., the angle between true north and magnetic north.

larly true in the noble voyage of Captain Martin Frobisher who, as you will see, has diligently observed this variation of the needle. And such observations of skilful pilots are the only way to explain it, for it surpasses the understanding of natural philosophy.

The making and using of maps, the shifting of sun and moon, and the use of the compass are common knowledge today, as are the use of the hour-glass for observing time, and the instruments of astronomy for finding latitude and longitude. Today, any mariner who has been to sea a couple of times is ashamed to come home if he is not able to render an account of these particulars. Because of this skill in navigation, it is now far easier for the people of Europe to make long voyages by sea than by land. Thus it has come to pass that within the memory of man—within these four score years—more new countries and regions have been discovered than in the previous five thousand. In fact, more than half the world has been discovered within the memory of men that are still living. When I speak of the world in this sense, I refer to the face or surface of the land and the sea which, uniting together, form a globe or sphere. Almighty God has given us this face of the earth as a most convenient place to inhabit, yet through negligence it has been so hidden and unknown that until recently man has lost the fruit and benefit of more than half the world.

It is a marvellous thing that man, who has always abhorred thraldom and restraint and has desired freedom so earnestly, should have been contented to be shut in by such narrow bounds for so many thousands of years. For it appears that in the past man has only known those countries that were joined together, or were separated by very narrow seas, as are Europe, Asia, and Africa. Between any of these, a man could travel either by land, or by finding some place where they are separated by very narrow seas and then sailing from one to the other without the art of navigation. He could do this by using landmarks, because the one land was within sight of the other. Even the mighty Hercules could do no more. Sweeping westward out of Greece, he conquered all the regions before him till he came to the strait that separates Spain and Barbary, which he said was the western edge of the world. There he erected two pillars as a perpetual monument to his fame. And to this day they are called the Pillars of Hercules, the one standing in Europe and the other in Africa, on both sides of the Straits of Gibraltar. Having come so far to the west, Hercules was contented, and said: "*Non plus ultra*"—no further.

In a similar fashion did Alexander the Great sweep out of Macedonia in Greece, passing through Armenia, Persia, and India till he came to the great river Ganges. And there he erected certain altars which are still called the Altars of Alexander, and these were reckoned as the eastern boundary of the world. Alexander knew that Asia extended somewhat farther to the east and northeast but thought that the countries lying in that direction were small and of little consequence. So no man passed beyond the Altars in those days, although we know now that Asia extends eastward for another twenty degrees. It stretches to the Eoum[2] Sea and the Straits of Anian, which our Captain Frobisher hopes to locate.

The southern parts of the world were described by Ptolemy, king of Egypt, who was more curious about the face of the earth than any king before him, or even after him until very recently. He described those parts towards Africa which are known only 16° beyond the equator. The southern boundary was called the Mountains of the Moon, out of which the mighty Nile River is supposed to flow. And on the north, Thule was called Ultima so long that it was esteemed a great error for man to imagine any land farther north than that. Thule may have been Iceland, but it is more likely that it was one of the Orkneys.

I have now described very briefly the four principal boundaries of the world, as they have been known from the beginning of time until these last eighty years: that is, the Straits of Gibraltar on the west, the Altars of Alexander on the east, Ultima Thule on the north, and 16° beyond the equator to the south. But the 16° of south latitude are known only in Africa, which extends no more than 70° in longitude. Whatever countries or regions lie beyond 180° in longitude, 60° in north latitude, and 16° in south latitude have been discovered in recent years through the efforts of many different people—Englishmen, Spaniards, Portuguese, Frenchmen, and Italians. These men, to their everlasting glory and renown, will soon have searched out and explored every remote corner of the world. Until recently the world was divided into three parts—Europe, Asia, and Africa. Today, however, the valour and industry of these men have added another three.

For the whole world can be divided first into two principal regions; the one is elemental, consisting of earth and water; the other is heavenly, consisting of fire and air. Although the heavenly regions are one, they have a diversity of motions: first, the Primary Motion or rotation around the arctic and antarctic poles; and second, that other motion of the orbs and planets which move around the poles of the zodiac. From this there arises the number of six substantial parts of the world—the four elements and the two varieties of motion. In the

2The South China Sea

same way, the inferior world, or surface of the earth, is also divided into six parts—Europe, Asia, Africa, Terra Septentrionalis, America, and Terra Australis. Because this division seems somewhat strange, I will briefly list their boundaries.

The Chief Boundaries of the Principal Parts of the World

Europe is bounded on the west by our Western Ocean, on the south by the Mediterranean Sea, and on the east by the Aegean Sea, the Black Sea, and the meridian northward from the mouth of the Tanais River.[3] On the north, the boundaries were formerly the Hebrides and Orkney Islands and the mountains of Sarmatia. By the explorations of the English, however, these boundaries are extended to the sea that surrounds Norway, Lapland, and Muscovy.

Africa is bounded on the west by the Atlantic Ocean, on the south by the South Ocean, which also passes beyond the Cape of Good Hope, on the east by the Red Sea, and on the north by the Mediterranean Sea.

Asia is bounded on the south by the South Ocean, on the east by the Mare Eoum and the Straits of Anian, on the north by the Scythian Sea, and on the west by the meridian of the Tanais River, and the Black, Aegean, and Red seas.

Terra Septentrionalis is divided from Asia by the Scythian Sea, from Europe by the North Sea about Iceland (this was formerly called the Mare Congelatum or Frozen Sea), and from America by Frobisher's Straits. It lies around the north pole and is contained by the parallel at 70° north latitude, as is described more fully in the world maps of Mercator and Ortelius.

This northern part of the world has been explored mainly through the industry of Englishmen. For as Mercator mentioned, there was a friar of Oxford, a great mathematician, who travelled very far north more than 200 years ago, and described almost all the land around the pole with an astrolabe. He found it divided into four parts by four great guts or channels. These channels deliver themselves into a monstrous cavern with such violence that any ship that enters one is doomed. It cannot be held back by the force of even the greatest wind but is swept headlong into that monstrous receptacle, and then into the bowels of the earth. The friar reports that the southwest part of that land is fruitful and wholesome. The northeast part (in respect to England) is

[3]The Don River

inhabited by a people called pygmies who, at most, are four feet high. One of the four monstrous channels follows the meridian of the Fortunate Islands. It has three mouths through which it receives the ocean, is frozen more than three months of the year, and is thirty-seven leagues wide. The next channel to the east lies beyond Vagats Island at 110° of longitude and receives the eastern ocean through five months. As it is swift and narrow, it is never frozen. The third gut is at 190° longitude and receives the eastern ocean through nineteen openings. The fourth channel is at 280°. All of these raging channels run directly towards a point under the north pole, where there is also said to be a monstrous mountain of wonderful great height and about thirty-five leagues in circumference at the base.

Guillaume Postel says that one of the best habitations for human beings is under and around the pole, for there they have continual daylight. But this seems contrary to the principles of the sphere, which show us that they should see the sun continuously for only half the year. This would occur when the sun was north of the equator, and between one equinox and the next; during the other half of the year, when the sun was south of the equator, the inhabitants would have continual darkness. But as Postel was a good astronomer, I doubt that he would question the teachings of the sphere. He meant, probably, that with the long twilights, the high swelling of the earth, and the high mountain under the pole, they would have continual light. However, I will discuss this more fully later on when I discuss the temperature of those northern regions. Such a detailed description of the polar regions suggests that the friar from Oxford was a very careful observer. It also increases the probability that the report of his voyage is truthful, for he measured and counted so diligently the width of the different channels, how long they were frozen, and through how many openings or mouths each of them received the ocean.

I have dwelt so long upon the description and boundaries of this part of the earth because I find that it was all discovered by the English. Although the greatest portion was described more than 200 years ago, yet parts of it were first explored by Sir Hugh Willoughby, Knight, an Englishman who ventured and lost his life in the cause and so died an honourable death. With him was Richard Chancellor, chief pilot for the 1554 voyage.[4] Chancellor discovered that Norway, Lapland, etc., were not joined to Greenland or to any other part of the northern land, and

---

[4]This was the first voyage undertaken by the "Russia" or "Muscovy" Company. Willoughby and Chancellor started their historic voyage from Ratcliffe in May (probably on May 10) 1553.

that a man might sail around them to Muscovy and then continue as far to the eastward as the great river Ob. And in his last three voyages, our worthy general, Captain Martin Frobisher, has discovered and described a great part of that land lying around the pole, particularly its southwest boundaries. He intends, God willing, to describe half of that land by sailing to Cathay through the northwest passage, and the other half as well, if he can find a path that will lead him back to England by the northeast. Such an undertaking is one of the weightiest matters in the world, and its successful completion will cause other princes to admire the fortunate condition and great valour of the English nation. But let us return to the boundaries of the other parts of the world.

America is an island that is bounded on the east by the Atlantic Ocean, on the west by the Pacific Ocean, on the south by the Straits of Magellan, and on the north by Frobisher's Straits.

Terra Australis seems to be a great, firm land lying under and about the south pole. In many places it is a fruitful land, but it is not yet thoroughly explored; it has been seen and visited only at a few places along its north coast by the Portuguese and Spaniards during their voyages to the East and West Indies. Most of it lies beyond 40° south latitude, yet in some places it thrusts out great promontories as far north as the tropic of Capricorn. The best known parts are opposite the Cape of Good Hope—where the Portuguese commonly see parrots of a wonderful bigness—and on the south side of the Straits of Magellan, where it is called Terra del Fuego. It is believed that this southern land that lies about the antarctic pole is far bigger than the land that lies around the arctic pole. But we have no proof of this because we have no general description of it, such as we have of the northern land.

I have now given the main boundaries of each of the six parts that the earth was recently divided into. So that this might be seen more clearly, I append a map of the world, drawn so that the viewer may see at a glance which parts are newly discovered and which parts have been known since ancient times. The newly discovered lands have been drawn with dotted lines, and the old lands with solid lines. Thus at one glance the reader can see the shape of the parts which make up the whole face of the earth. Although the map is but roughly framed, and without degrees of latitude and longitude, it will still serve the purpose for which it was made. My intention with both the map and the rest of this discourse on the three voyages of Captain Frobisher is to present a true but simple account of the whole matter. For if I were to entangle myself in fine words or eloquent phrases, I would merely betray my

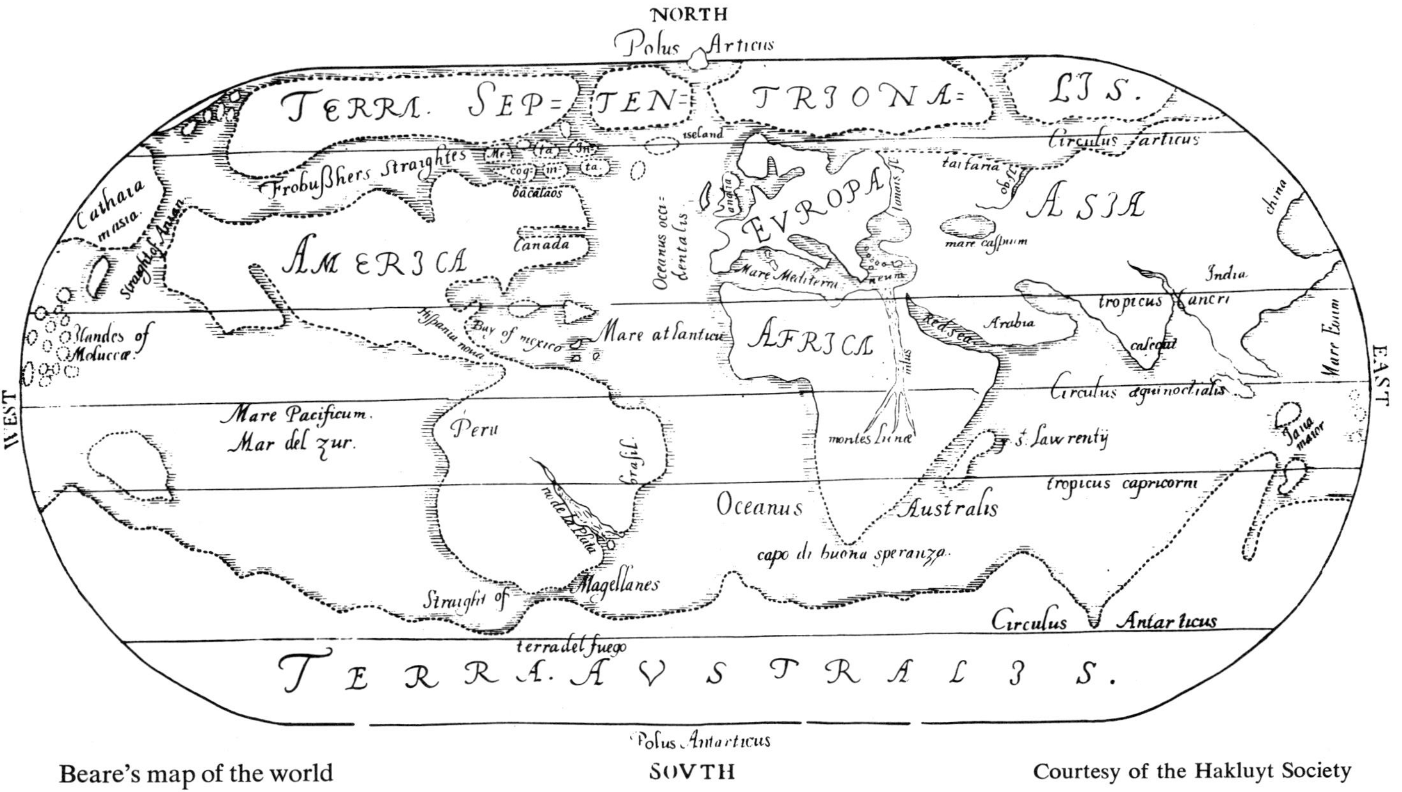

Beare's map of the world
    Courtesy of the Hakluyt Society

own ignorance and lack of education. Therefore you must look for nothing here but such plain talk and writing as soldiers and sailors use in their daily work. And this, of necessity, will be used by any man who will deal with such matters as these.

In this discourse and map, we can see the courage and achievements of modern men. Within the last eighty years, they have enlarged the boundaries of the known world to such an extent that we now have two or three times the space for our earthly wanderings that we had just a short time ago. As a result, men no longer need to strive contentiously for space to build a house, or for an acre or two of turf, when whole worlds offer themselves to any one who will possess, inhabit, and cultivate them. There are now entire continents, without owners or masters, that could bring forth all manner of corn and grain, all sorts of land animals such as horses, elephants, pigs, and sheep, a great variety of flying fowls like pheasants, partridges, quail, parrots, and ostriches, and all manner of fruits such as almonds, dates, quinces, pomegranates, and oranges which are wholesome, medicinal, and delectable. In many of these lands, a great variety of beautiful flowers spring forth, both winter and summer, that are sweet-smelling and comfortable. There is an abundance of fair hills furnished with all manner of woods and pleasant valleys, and strange beasts and fishes in both fresh and salt water. These lands also produce many kinds of metals such as gold, silver, and iron, as well as a variety of precious stones and spices. Anything that may be desired is there, be it for pleasure, profit, or necessity.

Because it is such an easy thing to acquire these lands, I would hope that the English do not overshoot themselves in refusing such opportunities, as they did in the time of Henry VIII. At that time, all of the West Indies were offered to the English, and only when they rejected them were the islands offered to Spain. And the Spaniards are still enjoying their treasures and commodities. In all later discoveries, however, the English have been as aggressive as any others. Initially, the boundaries of Europe were established by their northern voyages, for Ptolemy, Strabo, and all other geographers described them only as far north as the Orkney Islands and the mountains of Sarmatia. They knew that there was land north of Germany, Poland, Muscovy, and Asia, but they did not know whether the land was solid or whether it was divided by some sea or strait. This doubt has been long since resolved, however, through the valiant efforts of Sir Hugh Willoughby, Knight, who died an honourable death in searching for an answer to that question, as I mentioned earlier. And his explorations have since been completed by the Borough[5] brothers and other valiant young men, who sailed eastward beyond the mighty Ob River as far as the empire of the Great Khan of Tartary.

Sir Hugh's voyage was undertaken in an attempt to sail to Cathay by way of the northeast passage, a route which he considered feasible for the following reasons. First, he said, the horn of a unicorn was recently found near the mouth of the Ob River on the coast of Tartary. This could only have been carried there by sea, and from either India or Cathay, as those are the only places where unicorns are found. Second, a fisherman of Tartary reported that he had sailed very far to the southeast and found that the sea continued indefinitely. And finally, another Tartar who lived near the Scythian Sea reported that anything cast into that sea would be carried away to the westward by a steady current along the coast. Therefore there must be a passage to some larger sea to the west. Sir Hugh's voyage showed that the frozen zones were in fact not frozen, that man could both live in those northern lands and sail in those northern seas, in spite of the opinion of almost all the old philosophers. For in his voyage to Muscovy, his men sailed beyond 72° north latitude, while the frozen zone begins at 66½°. Although he failed to find a northeast passage to Cathay, having perished in the attempt, he did find a sea route to St. Nicholas,[6] which has been very beneficial to England. The trade through this northern route has helped to maintain the navy, in addition to yielding a good annual profit.

This northern voyage is known to be more dangerous and difficult than any the Spaniards or Portuguese have ever been involved with. For they are born in a country that has rather hot weather, and sail in similar temperatures; thus their voyages are easy, although they are frequently very long. I think it can be honestly said that in all their lengthy voyages to the Indies, they were never oppressed by such an infinite number and variety of dangers as were our valiant Captain Frobisher and his company in their three voyages. And yet they courageously persisted with the enterprise and will not cease—God willing—until they have found the passage to Cathay, to the everlasting glory and renown of England. In addition, it was through the valour of the English that Baccalaos[7] was discovered. For it was Sebastian

---

[5]Stephen Borough was master of Chancellor's ship, the *Edward Bonaventure* on the 1553 voyage; his younger brother, William, was a common seaman. Both brothers continued as navigators and officers in the Muscovy Company.

[6]At the mouth of the Dvina River in the White Sea

[7]Newfoundland

Cabot, an Englishman born in Bristol, who was the first Christian ever to set foot on that land. Having been furnished with ships, arms, and men by King Henry VII and sent forth to search for the northwest passage to Cathay, he went ashore in many places and brought home several people and many commodities of that country in token of possession. This same Englishman also discovered that other part of America that lies south of Brazil around the famous river called Rio de la Plata. The English have also made many voyages to Guinea and Benin, although the Spaniards and Portuguese, being closer, got there first and were able to prevent the English from building towns and fortresses. It would appear, then, that the long and dangerous navigations of the English have diligently and studiously explored the temperature of all the zones, regardless of whether they were hot, cold, or indifferent. These men have travelled from the north pole to the equator and, continuing south, have passed even beyond the tropic of Capricorn before they returned homeward. Therefore we are inferior to no other nation in undertaking long and notable voyages by sea. Nor is there any nation that is comparable to us in undertaking similar voyages by land.

For what nation has ever had such long trade routes by land as that of England into Persia. After sailing two months along the western and northern coasts of Norway and Lapland, and into the Bay of St. Nicholas,[8] there still remain some 3,000 English miles to be covered by land and fresh water. From the merchant's house in St. Nicholas to the city of Volugda is a distance of 700 miles along the rivers Dvina and Sughaua. From there to the city of Yearuslave on the Volga is an overland journey of 140 miles; then the traveller follows the mighty Volga eastward about 700 miles till it turns to the south and leads him to Astrakhan on the Caspian Sea, which is another 900 miles. A good steady wind will carry him across the Caspian Sea in two or three days to a port called Bilbill; and from there, he travels by camel for 600 miles—which takes twenty-one days—to the city of Tauris or Teuris, which is the greatest trading centre in Persia. This long and painful overland journey was made by Mr. Anthony Jenkinson,[9] a worthy gentleman who drew a map and wrote a detailed description of all of Muscovy, the first that I have ever

[8]The White Sea

[9]Jenkinson joined the Muscovy Company in 1557 as captain general of their fleet and their agent in Russia for three years. He made three subsequent trips to Russia, and was probably the first Englishman to visit Central Asia.

seen. And therefore the English are to be preferred above all other nations for making long voyages by land. The Spaniards and Portuguese are undoubtedly worthy of immortal fame and glory for their great undertakings and their great achievements; yet they have neither seen nor heard of such strange and wonderful things as have happened to the English. For neither Spaniard nor Portuguese ever saw the sun and moon make whole and perfect revolutions above the horizon, such as our men see every year during their voyage to Muscovy. When they stay at Wardhouse[10] for any length of time, they see the sun revolve continually in the sky for two months at a time, so that if they are not careful, they forget what day of the month it is, for they have no nights. Once every twenty-four hours, however, the sun drops down almost to the northern horizon, where it is commonly dimmed somewhat by thick fogs and vapours that rise from the earth. This approach of the sun to the northern horizon is considered their night and is enough for them to keep track of the days of the month.

But there is one inconvenience that dismays and deters most men, even the most courageous, from undertaking long voyages either by land or by sea, and that is fear of new elements, the extremes of heat and cold to which they are not accustomed. Many men think that if they travel far enough northward, they will be frozen to death in the congealed and frozen seas. And if they travel far enough south, they are afraid of being parched and broiled to death by the extreme heat of the middle burning zone. Should they escape with their lives, they would still be burned as black as coal, as are the Indians and Black Moors who live there. They are persuaded of this partly by the sight of the people themselves, and partly by the argument of certain philosophers who tried to prove that no one could live between the tropics of Cancer and Capricorn because of the extreme heat that would be engendered there by the continual beating of the sun. These philosophers would have us believe that the polar regions cannot be inhabited either, because the sun there is so far distant that the cold and snow have been increasing continually, as some think, since the beginning of the world. I will attempt now to refute this opinion, because I know from my own personal experience that it is wrong, and because I find that the course of the sun in the zodiac (which God has ordained to give illumination and life to all things) can induce no such extremes. And so, finally, I affirm that all parts of the world are habitable.

[10]The old fortress of Vardo, on an island off the coast of Lapland at 70°22′ N.

First, we know this through the experience of Captain Wyndham,[11] an Englishman who went to Guinea on a trading venture in 1553. He entered so far within the torrid zone that he was within 3° or 4° of the equator, stayed there some months, and returned with a profit. The following year, he made another profitable voyage to the coast of Benin, which is east of Guinea, and within three degrees of the equator. And yet it is certainly true that the entire coast between the Cape de las Palmas to the Isle of St. Thomas, which is directly under the equator, is subject to more smothering and blooming heat, infections, and contagious airs, than any other place in the entire torrid zone. But the cause of this is not the climate itself but some accidents or irregularities of the land. For it is certain that things like mountains, seas, forests, and lakes may, through the way they are situated, bring about strange and extraordinary effects which the climate itself would never produce.

I mention these voyages of the English, not to show how ready they are to undertake long and dangerous voyages, but to demonstrate that the torrid zone can be, and is, inhabited. We have amongst us in England many Moors and Ethiopians from all parts of the torrid zone: in a short time, they learn to endure the cold of our country, so why should we be unable to bear the heat of theirs? But there is no need of further examples, for the entire coasts of Guinea and Benin are inhabited by Portuguese, Spaniards, Frenchmen, and even a few Englishmen, who have built castles and towns there. I will say this, however, to the London merchants who engage in an annual trade with Morocco. It is certain that the greater part of the torrid zone in June is cooler and far more temperate than Morocco, as the following arguments and experiences will demonstrate.

Let us consider the breadth of this torrid zone. As is well known, this is a band that extends 23½° on either side of the equator. Its total breadth, then, is 47°, and it stretches from the tropic of Capricorn on the south to the tropic of Cancer on the north. Imagine, now, two other parallels, one 20° south of the equator, the other 20° north. It will be clear that the sun crosses each of these parallels twice a year. I shall now demonstrate by both logic and experience that the area between the two parallels—40° of latitude—can not only be inhabited, but is most fruitful and delectable; if any place suffers from an extremity of heat, that place cannot be within that space of 20° on either side of the equator, but must be under or around the two

[11]Frobisher's first sea voyage was as a member of the ill-fated Wyndham expedition when he was 14 or 15 years old.

tropics. And the closer you approach to either of the tropics, the more you are exposed to an extremity of heat, so that Morocco, some 6° or 7° from the tropic of Cancer, will be hotter than any place at or near the equator.

First, thousands of travellers and merchants tell us that the East and West Indies, as well as many other places near the equator, abound with all sorts of grain, herbs, grass, fruit, wood, and cattle that we have here in England, and thousands more besides. In addition, they are far more wholesome and delectable than what we have in these northern climes, as will be obvious to anyone who reads the accounts of those who have travelled to Arabia, India, the Islands of Molucca, or America, all of which are situated near the middle of the torrid zone. Everyone who has ever been there agrees that this torrid zone has the greenest meadows and plains and the fairest mountains and valleys of any place on earth. In addition, it has goodly rivers stocked with all manner of fish, and thick, green woods that bear fruit throughout the whole year. And gold, silver, and spices abound, together with delectable fruits in such abundance that people now believe the earthly paradise must lie either at or very near the equator.

The philosophers of old stated that nothing could prosper in the torrid zone because of the extreme heat that would be generated by a sun that was continually overhead. The reports of recent visitors to that region will therefore appear strange unless I support them with natural causes and substantial reasons. First, you must understand that the amount of heat which any place on earth receives from the sun depends on two things. One is the angle that the sun's rays make with the surface of the earth; for example, these rays strike the torrid zone at right angles and the zones about the poles at very oblique angles. The other is the length of time the sun continues above the horizon. There is most heat, then, where the sun shines most directly down and at the same time abides a great period above the horizon. If either of these is diminished, the heat becomes less intense. It is this second influence, the time that the sun abides above the horizon, that was forgotten by the philosophers of old. They remembered only the angle that the sun's rays make with the surface of the earth. If this was a right angle, as it is in the torrid zone, then more heat was generated: if this was an oblique angle, as it is towards both the north and south poles, then less heat was generated. Now these are good and substantial arguments, for the perpendicular beams reflect and reverberate among themselves, so that every beam strikes the earth twice and thus doubles the heat. In our own latitude of 50° or 60°, however, the sun's rays descend obliquely, strike the earth but once, and then depart; as a result, they generate less heat. On the other hand, the sun abides longer above the horizon at our latitude than it does at the equator and thus increases the amount of heat. During the summer, the sun will sometimes abide in our sky for sixteen or eighteen hours, while at the equator it is always twelve. Our nights, meanwhile, are but six or eight hours long, while those at the equator—like the days—are always twelve. And thus it comes to pass, through the advantages of long days and short nights, that the heat here in summer is as great as theirs. This has been proved through experience and is quite consistent with sound reasoning. Therefore, if someone could find out how much heat is generated by the angle of the sun's rays, and how that heat is increased as the sun abides longer above the horizon, he could then tell how much heat and how much cold there is in all the regions of the earth.

The cold regions of the world are those which tend towards the arctic and antarctic poles and lie beyond the bounds of the seven climates.[12] This is clearly set forth by Johannes de Sacrobosco,[13] who declared that all that part of the world which is beyond the seventh climate, or north of the 50th parallel of latitude, is discommodious and intolerable. But Gemma Frisius[14], a more recent writer, finding that England and Scotland were beyond the seventh climate, and knowing them to be very temperate, added two other climates which reached to 56° north. In this way he increased the first computation to embrace England, Scotland, Denmark, Muscovy, etc., which are all rich and mighty kingdoms.

I will now attempt to prove, therefore, that all of the land lying beyond the last climate, including that at the very poles, is or may be inhabited, especially by such creatures as are bred and engendered

[12]Technically, a "climate" was a zone or band running around the earth and bounded by parallels of latitude. The parallels delimiting the "climates" were spaced so that the amount of daylight on any two adjacent lines varied by half-an-hour on the longest day of the year. The ancient geographers theoretically divided both the northern and southern hemispheres into twenty-four such climatic zones, but they were acquainted with only nine of them, which they named after the principal cities situated within them. Thus they spoke of the "climates" of Alexandria, Rhodes, Rome, etc. The climate of Rome was the fifth one north of the equator.

[13]John Holywood or Halifax, a Jesuit priest, educated at Oxford. One of the outstanding mathematicians of the 13th century, and author of the famous *Tractatus de Sphaera.*

[14]The most influential Dutch mathematician of the 16th century. Born 1508; died on May 25, 1558, at Louvain, where he was a professor of medicine.

there. For it must be confessed that a particular creature cannot live in every region, especially with the same joy and felicity as it did where it was born. This natural agreement between a place and a thing bred in that place is well illustrated by the elephant. If we remove it from its natural place, it may still live, but it will never engender or bring forth young. The same is true of many plants and herbs. The orange tree, for example, brings forth abundant fruit at Naples, while at Rome and Florence it bears no fruit at all but only fair green leaves. When it is transplanted into England, it barely stays alive till the next winter, when it is pinched and withered with cold. Yet it does not follow from this that Rome, Florence, and England can not be inhabited.

In demonstrating that the cold regions of the earth are suitable for human habitation, I shall be very brief, because the same arguments have already been advanced to show that the middle zone is temperate. They are derived from the fact that all heat and cold proceed from the sun by reason of either the angle that the sun's beams make with the horizon, or the length of time that the sun abides above the horizon each day.

It must be understood that the closer a man is to the equator, the higher the sun will rise over his head each day at noon. But there the sun remains a shorter time above the horizon, causing shorter days, with longer and cooler nights. In the regions about either pole, on the other hand, the sun does not rise so high above the horizon, but abides longer in the sky and thus makes longer days with short warm nights. We also know from experience that summer nights in Scotland and Gothland can be very hot, while those at the equator are occasionally quite cool. The heat that is generated by the longer days continues to increase as you draw nearer to the pole. It is greatest at the pole itself, where the sun remains above the horizon for six months at a time, making the day to be half a year long.

And surely divine providence would have arranged all things so that one way or another everything could be employed to some purpose. This is particularly true here on earth, where man was given dominion over all things. Therefore we need have no doubt that the region about the pole is temperate and commodious during the summer. But the controversy is mainly concerned with the winter, for during that period the sun leaves the sky and is seen no more for six months. Some people believe that during this time the region must be deformed with horrible darkness and continual night. As a result, animals would not be able to seek their food, and the cold would become intolerable. Through these two evils, all living creatures would be constrained to die, and thus the region about the pole should be desolate and uninhabited.

These objections, however, may be answered in this manner. Although it is true that the sun is absent from the polar regions for six months at a time, it does not necessarily follow that the darkness should be so extreme. For the sun travels but a short distance below their horizon, and thus the day is prolonged by twilight. Later on, the residue of the night receives additional light from the moon and stars until the new day arrives. For these reasons, their nights are seldom as dark as they are near the equator, where the twilights are short and the nights are darker than in any other place on earth. We know that during a summer night in England we can travel all night by the light of the moon and stars, and could do many other things as well if it were necessary. There is also no doubt whatever that our cattle can see well enough to eat at night, even though our nights should be darker than they are at the pole. Thus we may testify that the summers are warm and fruitful at the pole, and even the nights of winter are tolerable to living creatures.

And though it be true that the time of darkness there is very cold, nature has not failed to provide for her creatures. The beasts are covered with hair that grows thicker as the violence of the cold increases, and for this reason the best and richest furs are found in the coldest regions. The birds, too, have thicker skins and feathers and a greater quantity of down than they do in warmer regions. Our countrymen who go trading to St. Nicholas or fishing to Wardhouse tell us that far beyond the Arctic circle, and throughout all those northern seas, they find the largest number of great fishes such as whales, as well as an abundance of mean fishes such as herring, cod, haddock, brettes, etc. All of which argues that both the sea and the land are thickly populated in the arctic countries.

Some people will be amazed, perhaps, to hear of such temperate places in the arctic regions, when our Captain Frobisher and his company were troubled by so many mountains of floating ice and by such cold and stormy weather. He also reported that there was always snow on the tops of the mountains, and that the soil was so barren that neither woods nor trees would grow there, but only some low shrubs. To such objections we may point out that those infinite islands of drifting ice were engendered and congealed in the winter, but were thawed by the great heat of summer. Only then were they driven to and fro by the tides, winds, and currents to trouble the fleet. Actually, they show how great is the heat of summer in that region when it can thaw such monstrous blocks of ice. As for continual snow on the tops of mountains, this also happens in the tropics because there is not sufficient space for the sun's reflections, which would normally melt the snow. The cold, stormy winds and barrenness of the country are the same as we have in Cornwall and Devonshire, where neither tree nor hedge will grow within seven or eight miles of the north coast, although we know those parts to be fruitful and fertile. The cause of this is the cold north winds which sweep in from the sea and are so sharp and bitter that they kill all young and tender plants. And so it is in the islands of Meta Incognita, which are subject mostly to east and northeast winds. Last year, in fact, these winds choked up the passage with so much ice that the ships could hardly reach their destination. In spite of any objections that might be raised, however, the country is inhabited by men, women, and children and a great variety and number of beasts such as bears, deer, hares, foxes, and dogs. There is also a great number of birds such as ducks, seamews, wilmots, partridges, larks, crows, and hawks.

It appears, then, that not only is the middle zone suitable for habitation, but the polar zone as well. This was thoroughly understood by Captain Frobisher through his study of the sphere and of all other subjects pertaining to the art of navigation, as well as through his years of experience both by land and by sea. He was persuaded that there was a different and shorter route to Cathay than the one that the Portuguese followed each year around the Cape of Good Hope. After much planning and conferring with his friends, he laid before them a chart which showed that such a voyage by the northwest was not only possible but easy. He was determined, moreover, to prove it, to bring back positive evidence that he had found a northwest route to Cathay, or not to return at all. He knew that such a project was one of the few things left in the whole world by which a man of vision might be made famous and fortunate. Although he was very anxious to perform such a notable act, he had absolutely no means at his disposal; he did have great expectations, however, which were supported by some secret intelligence that I had best leave unexplained. For a long time, Frobisher discussed these matters with his friends, and tried for over fifteen years to obtain the support of a number of merchants, but found that they would never consider even the most virtuous enterprise unless it involved sure, certain, and immediate gains. Finally, he repaired to the court, where he laid his entire plan before the noble and learned men assembled there. Among many men who favoured his honest and commendable enterprise, he was particularly beholden to the Right Honourable Ambrose Dudley, Earl of Warwick, who has always been willing to support honourable actions and the men who plan them.

With the support of that honourable lord, Captain Frobisher began to receive some backing till, little by little, and with considerable personal expense and effort, he gathered together some adventurers who agreed to finance the expedition. He then prepared two small barks, the *Gabriel* and the *Michael*, of twenty-five and twenty tons respectively, and a small pinnace of ten tons burden, furnished them with provisions for twelve months, and sailed from Blackwall on June 15, 1576. Sailing northwest from England on July 1, he finally sighted a high rugged land which he judged to be Friesland,[15] but did not dare to approach it too closely because of the vast quantity of ice that lay along the coast and the thick fogs that they found so troublesome. Not far from there he lost sight of the pinnace, which must have been swallowed up by the sea during a great storm. With the pinnace he lost only four men. During that same storm, the *Michael* headed back towards England, where she eventually arrived with the report that Frobisher, too, had been lost. Although his topmast was blown overboard and his mast was sprung, Frobisher ignored these discomforts and continued his course to the northwest, knowing that the sea at length must have an ending and that some land should have a beginning that way. He was determined, therefore, to find out exactly what lands and seas there might be in that northwestern region where no man had explored before.

On July 20 he sighted a high headland which he named Queen Elizabeth's Foreland in honour of Her Majesty. Sailing north from there, he discovered another foreland. Between the forelands, and dividing them into two mainlands or continents, was a great bay or passage tightly packed with drifting ice. Our captain hoped to continue his exploration to the north but was detained opposite the entrance to the bay or passage by head-winds. Within a few days he noticed that the ice was gone; so he decided to see how deep the bay or passage was and to find out if it might perhaps lead him into some open sea on the other side. He entered the strait on July 21 and followed it for about fifty leagues, with a mainland or continent on either side. As he sailed westward, he decided that the land on his right side was the

---

[15]One of the many imaginary islands that first appeared in the North Atlantic with the publication of the Zeno brothers' map of 1558. Frobisher was actually off the east coast of Greenland.

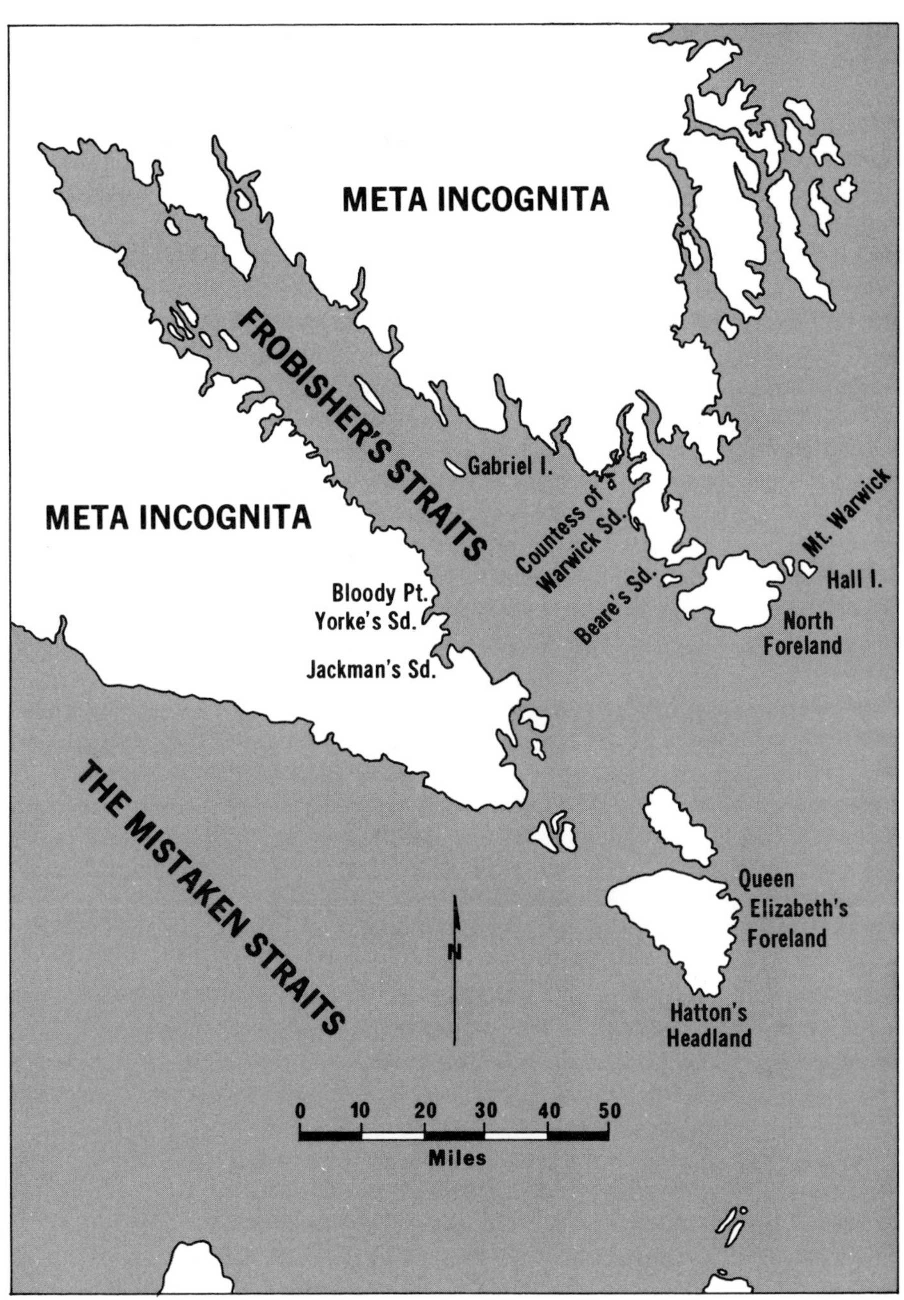

"Frobisher's Straits"

continent of Asia, while that on his left was the mainland of America.

This passage he named Frobisher's Straits in the same way that Magellan had named his strait at the southwest end of the earth. For when Magellan discovered a passage that divided America from the land that lies under the south pole—a passage that led to the south sea—he named it Magellan's Straits. After Frobisher had passed sixty leagues into his strait, he returned to its mouth, where he went ashore and found evidence that someone had built a fire, and many other tokens of the people who lived there. He also saw mighty deer that seemed almost human, for they pursued him so that he was forced to defend himself and narrowly escaped with his life.

On one occasion he was on the top of a hill when he saw a number of small things floating in the sea a long way away. He thought they were porpoises, seals, or some kind of strange fish, until they came closer, when he discovered that they were men in small boats made of leather. Before he could get down from the hill, some of them had almost cut him off from his boat, having sneaked through the rocks for that purpose. But our captain hurried to the shore, pulled on his hauberk, and just managed to save both himself and his boat.

Later on, he met these native people on many occasions. Sometimes they would come aboard his ship, bringing salmon and raw flesh which they would greedily devour before the astonished faces of the men. To show their agility, they tried many stunts upon the ropes of the ship, as our sailors do, and seemed to have very strong arms and nimble bodies. With our men, they exchanged coats of seal skins and bear skins and similar objects, for bells, looking-glasses, and other toys. After many courteous meetings with the natives, our men began to trust them, which was contrary to the captain's orders. Finally, five of our men were going ashore when their boat was intercepted by the natives, and they were never heard of again.

Having lost the five men in the boat, the captain scarcely had enough men left to take his vessel back to England. Nor could he go ashore himself to rescue the men, if that were possible, for he had no other boat. And the subtle traitors who had captured our men were now so wary that they would not come within our grasp. The captain, however, was very anxious to carry home some token of his having been to a newly discovered land, and was greatly disappointed that he had not apprehended some of the natives earlier. However, he devised a scheme that would deceive the deceivers. Knowing how greatly they delight in our toys, and especially in our bells, he rang a lowbell and indicated that he would give it to whoever would come to fetch it. Because the natives were afraid to come too close, he flung the bell towards them, but he purposely threw it short so that it would fall into the sea and be lost. To make them more greedy, he then rang a louder bell till one of the natives came to the side of the ship to receive it. Just as the man was about to take it from the captain's hand, he was thereby taken himself. For the captain suddenly dropped the bell, grabbed the man, and plucked him out of the sea by main force, boat and all, and into the ship. When he found himself in captivity, the man was so overcome with anger and disdain that he bit his tongue in twain within his mouth. He did not die, however, but lived till he got to England, where he died of a cold that he caught at sea.

This new prey was sufficient witness of Frobisher's distant and tedious voyage to unknown parts of the world. For no one had ever before seen or heard of such a strange infidel, nor could anyone understand his language. So, with this proof of his discoveries, Captain Frobisher sailed for home, arriving in England in August 1576, where he was highly commended by everyone for his great and noble effort. He was particularly applauded for the great hope he brought of the passage to Cathay. For he had no doubt whatever that he had found it and could pass freely through it, somewhere in those parts.

It will be remembered that when he first arrived at the mouth of his strait, Frobisher found so much ice along the coast that he could hardly get a boat ashore. After many attempts, he told his men that if any of them were successful in getting ashore, they were to bring him anything they could find, either living or dead, stick or stone, in token of Christian possession. These he would accept on behalf of the Queen's Most Excellent Majesty. Some of the company brought flowers, some green grass, and one man brought a piece of black stone, much like a seacole in colour, which seemed, because of its weight, to be some kind of metal or mineral. At first sight, the captain thought it of no importance and kept it only as a curiosity.

After his return to London, his friends kept asking him for souvenirs of the new country till he had nothing left to give them but pieces of the black stone. One of the pieces was given to a gentlewoman, the wife of one of the adventurers. By chance, she threw it into the fire, where it burned so long that when it was taken out and quenched in a little vinegar, it glistened with a bright marquesset of gold. After some discussion, the stone was taken to some goldfiners in London to be assayed and was found to contain large quantities of gold. The same goldfiners promised that there would be great profits if any quantity of the ore could be found, and offered to raise some of the necessary cash for continuing the search. And some that considered the matter most hopeful tried secretly to secure a lease of the mining areas at Her Majesty's hands, and thus to divert a great public profit to their own private gains.

In conclusion, the hope of finding more of the gold-bearing ore kindled a great urge in the hearts of many people to send forth another expedition. Preparations were therefore made for another voyage to the northwest the following year. And the captain was specifically commissioned to search for the gold-bearing ore rather than to continue his search for the northwest passage to Cathay. With a number of resolute and determined gentlemen, Captain Frobisher then called upon Her Majesty, who was lying at the house of the Right Honourable the Earl of Warwick, in Essex. When they left, they kissed Her Highness' hands, and with gracious countenance and comfortable words they departed towards their charges.

End of the First Voyage.

1577

The Second Frobisher Voyage

Who so maketh Navigations to these countries, hath
not only extreme winds, and furious Seas, to encounter withall, but also many monstrous and great
Islands of ice: a thing both rare, wonderful and
greatly to be regarded.

Dionyse Settle, 1577

1577

The Second Frobisher Voyage

A True Report of such Things as Happened in
THE SECOND VOYAGE OF CAPTAIN FROBISHER,
Intended for the Discovery of a new Passage to
Cathay, China, and the East Indies, by the Northwest.
A.D. 1577

On May 25, in the year of our Lord 1577, Captain Frobisher and the rest of his company boarded the ships which were riding at Blackwall, intending—with God's help—to sail with the first wind and tide. One of his ships was the *Aid*, a 200-ton vessel supplied by Her Majesty; the other two were small barks of some thirty tons each, the *Gabriel* and the *Michael*, suitably appointed with men, munitions, victuals, and all other things necessary for the voyage.

Aboard the admiral[1]—the *Aid*—were 100 men of all sorts, of which at least thirty were gentlemen and soldiers, and the rest competent and stalwart sailors. Aboard the *Gabriel*—the vice-admiral—were six soldiers and twelve sailors, and aboard the *Michael* were five soldiers and eleven sailors.

Aboard the *Aid* were:

General of the whole Company	Martin Frobisher
His Lieutenant	George Best
His Auncient (ensign?)	Richard Philpot
Corporal of the Shot	Francis Forder
The Rest of the Gentlemen	Henry Carew
	Edmund Stafford
	John Lee
	— Harvie
	Mathew Kynersley

[1]The flagship

<table>
<tr><td></td><td>Abraham Lyons</td></tr>
<tr><td></td><td>Robert Kynersley</td></tr>
<tr><td></td><td>Frauncis Brackenburye</td></tr>
<tr><td></td><td>William Armshaw</td></tr>
<tr><td>The Master</td><td>Christofer Hall</td></tr>
<tr><td>The Mate</td><td>Charles Jackman</td></tr>
<tr><td>The Pilot</td><td>Andrew Dyer</td></tr>
<tr><td>The M. Gunner</td><td>Richard Cox</td></tr>
</table>

Aboard the *Gabriel* were:

Captain	Edward Fenton
One Gentleman	William Tamfield
The Master	William Smith

Aboard the *Michael* were:

Captain	Gilbert Yorke
One Gentleman	Tho. Chamberlain
The Master	James Beare

On Whitsunday, May 26, 1577, we weighed anchor at Blackwall in the early morning and fell with the tide down to Gravesend, where we stayed till Monday night. The next morning, aboard the *Aid*, the minister of Gravesend offered us all communion and prepared us, as good Christians, to meet our God, and as resolute men to meet any fortune that might befall us. Then, that evening, we departed for Tilbury Hope.

On Tuesday, May 28, we arrived at Harwich in Essex about nine o'clock at night, where we stayed until Friday the thirty-first to take on certain victuals which we still needed. During that period some letters arrived from the Lords of the Council telling our general that he was not, under any circumstances, to increase his complement of men above the appointed number of 120. He therefore discharged many decent men, who departed most reluctantly. He also dismissed all of the condemned prisoners whom he had brought along, and who he thought would be essential for the success of the expedition. And then, as night was falling, he put to sea again on the thirty-first, sailing northward along the east coast of England and Scotland.

On June 7 we arrived at St. Magnus Sound in the Orkney Islands (called the Orcades in Latin), where we anchored on the south side of the bay. When our men went ashore, the inhabitants of the islands fled as from an enemy. The lieutenant therefore warned the men to stay together, while he went into the houses to explain who we were and why we were there. As soon as this was understood, the people entertained us in their humble but friendly manner and sold us such things as they had. While we were there, our assayers located a silver mine. Orkney is the main island of the Isles of Orcades and is located at 59½ ° north latitude. The country is very cold, as is normal for such a latitude, but still yields some fruit, and sustenance enough for people who are content to live so poorly. They have plenty of poultry and a good supply of eggs, fish, and fowl. For bread they eat oaten cakes, and for drink they have ewes' milk and ale. Their houses look very poor from the outside and sluttish from the inside, an appearance which agrees very well with the nature of the people. As most of the island is devoid of wood, the natives use heath and turf for fuel. Leather is extremely scarce in the Orcades, and the natives prefer old shoes or even old clothes and ropes in payment for their victuals, although they are not ignorant of the value of money. Today, the chief town is called Kyrway.[2] On the west side of the island there was formerly an abbey or religious house named Saint Magnus, which gave its name to the sound through which we passed. During our visit their governor, Lord Robert Steward, was imprisoned in Edinburgh by order of the regents of Scotland.

After we had laid in enough provisions for the voyage, we set sail on the night of June 8, passing through St. Magnus Sound before a merry wind; and dropping the land astern, we kept our course west-northwest for two days. Then the wind shifted so that we lay between the seas, but still made good our course to the westward, more or less, and occasionally made some northing as the wind shifted. It was there that we met three sail of English fishermen, homeward bound from Iceland, and had them carry some letters to our friends in England. For twenty-six days we sailed that sea without sighting any land, though we met with much driftwood and even whole trees. We also saw many monstrous fish, and some strange birds which must spend all their time at sea because they are so far from land.

At length God favoured us with more prosperous winds. And after we had sailed for four days with the wind at our stern, the *Michael*, which was in the lead, fired one of her guns and struck her sails, thinking she had sighted land on that fourth day of July. Because of the heavy mist they could not see very clearly, but both our dead reckoning and a great change in the appearance of the water, which suddenly became blacker and smoother, plainly indicated that we were not far from the coast. The general sent his master aboard the *Michael*—where he

[2]Kirkwall

had been the year before—with instructions to move in closer to see if they had, in fact, reached the coast. He could not see any land but saw many huge islands of ice, which we judged to be not more than twelve leagues from shore. Then, about ten o'clock that night, July 4, the weather suddenly cleared and we could see a land which we recognized as Friesland. When we checked our latitude and found that it was 60½ ° north, we knew that we were at the southernmost part of that land.

Friesland is a high, rugged land with its mountains almost completely covered with snow, and with so much drifting ice along its coast that it seems almost inaccessible. It is thought to be an island and is almost as big as England. It is called West Friesland, I believe, because it is farther west than any part of Europe. According to a description left us by two brothers,[3] the Venetians Nicholaus and Antonius Genoa, this land extends very far to the north. The Genoa brothers, the first known Christians to visit this land, were carried here from the coasts of Ireland, and shipwrecked almost 300 years ago. They charted every part of the coast and described the condition of its inhabitants, who were found to be as civil and religious as we are. We compared the Venetians' chart with that part of the coast we followed and found them to agree very well.

Fishing seems to be very good along this coast, for we dropped an unbaited hook in the water when we were lying becalmed, and soon caught a large fish called a halibut. It was so big that it furnished a day's supply of meat for the entire crew. Incidentally, this fish can be dangerous if you eat too much at one sitting. When we took soundings about five leagues off shore, the tallow in our sounding lead brought up a variety of coral that was almost white, and small stones as bright as crystal. Beyond any doubt, this land would prove to be very rich and beneficial once it was thoroughly explored, even though we saw no creature there but some small birds. It was a marvellous thing to behold the size of some of the icebergs we saw; besides that part which rose high above us, they extended as much as seventy or eighty fathom below the surface and were more than half a mile in circumference. And all this ice was fresh to the taste; it seems to be generated in the sounds of the area, or in some land near the pole, and driven along the coast by the winds and tides. Because we found none of this ice to taste salty, it would appear that it is not congealed of the water in the ocean sea, which is always salty. It must be bred in some quiet lakes, or in some great body of fresh water near the shore that is fed and replenished by melted snow from the mountain tops, or by rivers from the land.

[3]The Zeno brothers

When this intermingles with the sea-water, it is so extremely cold that it may cause some part of the salt water to freeze with it, but otherwise the ocean sea does not freeze; and therefore there is no Mare Glaciale or frozen sea, as was formerly believed.

On two occasions the general tried to land there, but because of sudden fogs, which are very common along that coast, he was afraid of being separated from his ship. As he was also threatened by the drifting ice, he was forced to return aboard his ship and give up his attempts at landing until some better opportunity should present itself. Having spent four days and nights sailing along that coast, and finding it to be bitterly cold and beset with continual mists, the general decided to leave immediately for Frobisher's Straits. This strait was named after the general, who was the first explorer who ever passed beyond 50° north, and who has discovered everything that is known for sure about Newfoundland, or, as it is also called, the continent or firm land of America. He discovered the strait last year, 1576, and hopes to find a through passage that way into the sea which lies on the back side of America. Through that sea, called Mare Pacificum or Mare de Sur, we could travel to Cathay, China, the East Indies, and all the dominions of the Great Khan of Tartary.

Between Friesland and the straits, we had a bad storm, which damaged the *Michael*, smashing her steerage and blowing her topmasts overboard. At this point, we were no more than fifty leagues from the straits according to our reckoning, so we struck our sails and lay a-hull[4] because we were afraid that with a northeast wind the storm might continue for days. We got separated from the barks during the storm but fortunately met them again on July 17. The previous evening, we had seen so many icebergs that we knew we were not far from land. Then, in the morning, the general sighted land from the maintop during a break in the weather. As he was not certain of our position, however, he sent the two barks off in opposite directions to see if they could locate either the north or the south foreland. The *Aid*, meanwhile, lay off and on at sea, near a large iceberg which marked our rendezvous. Then, about noon, when the weather cleared up a little, we could see quite clearly the North Foreland, or Hall's Land, as it is called. We could also see Hall's Island, where we mined the ore that was taken back to England last year, 1576. These places were named after Christopher Hall, who was present when the ore was located and mined; at that time he was master of Captain Frobisher's bark, the *Gabriel*. When we first arrived, the seas along that coast were so thickly covered with huge

[4]That is, with sails furled and helm lashed a-lee.

slabs of drifting ice that we thought they alone might deserve the name of Mare Glaciale, and be called the Icy Sea. The North Foreland is believed to be separated from the northern continent by a little sound called Hall's Sound. This North Foreland, or Hall's Island, is about the size of the Isle of Wight and stands at the entrance to the strait on the north side. Its latitude is 62° 50′ north.

God had blessed us with a happy landfall, so we headed into the straits, which lead a little north of west, keeping as close to the shore as the ice would permit. On July 18 the general took the goldfiners to Hall's Island in a small rowing pinnace to see if he could find any more of the ore they had found the previous year. But on the whole island they could not find a piece as large as a walnut. Thus it would seem to be a miracle of God that, with only one rich deposit on the entire island, it should have been found by an Englishman. Apparently it was God's will and pleasure to have our country enriched with no less abundance of his treasures and gold mines than any other nation, and to have the faith of his gospel and holy name published and enlarged through all those corners of the earth, and amongst all those idolatrous infidels. The men who had been searching the neighbouring islands, meanwhile, found that they all had rich ore deposits. When our general heard these good tidings, he returned to his ship about ten o'clock at night and was joyfully welcomed with a volley of shot. He brought with him some eggs, fowl, and young seals which the men had collected on the island.

The men had found snares set to catch birds, some freshly cut sticks, and other signs that the natives had visited the islands fairly recently. The general therefore made plans for the safety of his company, for he had learned during his first voyage of the subtle and cruel disposition of those people.

On Friday, July 19, the general went ashore early in the morning with forty of his gentlemen and soldiers. He wanted to explore the island, examine the habitations of the natives, and find a suitable harbour for the ships. Because the ice was so thick along the coast that they could hardly pick their way through it, they had great difficulty in getting ashore, but finally managed to reach Hall's Land. They found a good quantity of ore there as well as on the other small islands. Leaving the boats well guarded on the beach, the general and his men went inland for about two English miles to the top of a high hill. There they built a column or cross of stones piled up neatly to a fair height, then sounded a trumpet and solemnly prayed while they kneeled around a flag. They honoured the place with the name of Mount Warwick in memory of the Right Honourable the Lord Ambrose Dudley, Earl of

Warwick, whose noble spirit and good countenance in this, as in all other fine actions, offered great encouragement and assistance. When their ceremonies were ended, they started back towards their boats, as they saw nothing worthy of further exploration in a country that seemed totally barren and littered with ragged, snow-covered mountains. And while they were marching towards the boats, they noticed some of the natives on top of Mount Warwick waving at them with a flag and making a great noise with cries like the lowing of bulls. The natives seemed very anxious to confer with our people, and so the general, who understood them best, answered with similar cries and with the blare of our trumpets. At the sound they seemed to rejoice, skipping, laughing, and dancing for joy.

By holding up two fingers and by sending two of our men to meet them part way, we suggested that they should also send two envoys. They understood us and immediately sent two of their men to meet ours. The four men met at a discreet distance from any of the others, and without having any weapons with them. Our men gave them pins, points, and such other trifles as they had, while they gave our men two bow cases and a few lesser things. They earnestly requested our men to go with them into the interior of their country, and our men offered them similar hospitality aboard the ships. But it seems that neither party trusted the other enough to visit them in their own territory.

The natives trade in this manner. Taking the things they mean to trade, they place them on the ground. Then they back away, watching to make certain that the people with whom they hope to trade will place their merchandise on the ground and then back away in a similar fashion. Then, if they like what has been offered, the first traders will come forward and take it; if not, they will take their own goods and leave.

By now the day was almost over, so we hurried back to the boats, intending to search along the coast for some harbour for our ships. This was becoming urgent, for they had been standing off and on in the channel between the two lands all the while, where they were exposed to the danger of the floating ice which surrounded them, as well as to the sudden gusts of wind which occur so frequently along that coast.

When the natives saw that we were leaving, they earnestly and affectionately called us back again, following us almost to our boats. And so the general and the master, who understood the manners of those people better than the rest of us, went to meet two of them apart from the others. If he could catch them, the general meant to carry them forcibly aboard his ship. He wanted to give certain toys and clothing to one of them, and then release him with every sign of courtesy; the other he would keep for an interpreter. When the four of them met together, they first exchanged a few things, and then one of the natives who had nothing left to trade cut off the tail of his coat, which they consider a very fine ornament, and gave it to the general as a present.

Then, at a signal, our two seized the two natives. But they were on the side of a hill, and as the ground was slippery because of the snow, they lost their grip. Their prey escaped, running nimbly away to recover bows and arrows, which they had hidden not far behind them in the rocks. Although they were the only natives in sight, they still pursued and assaulted our general and his master with great fury and desperation. They chased them back towards the boats and wounded the general in the buttocks as he retreated, which he did because he was unarmed, and because he suspected that there were more of the natives hidden behind the rocks. The soldiers who were guarding the boats heard the general calling for assistance and hurried to his rescue, thinking that he was being pursued by great numbers of savages. At the sound of one of our calivers, the natives discharged their arrows, then fled, with our men in hot pursuit.

A servant of my Lord of Warwick, called Nicholas Conger, who was a good runner and unencumbered with any furniture besides a dagger at his back, overtook one of them. Being a Cornishman and a good wrestler, he showed that native such a Cornish trick that he made his sides ache against the ground for a month afterward. And so the one was taken alive and carried away, but the other escaped. With their strange new captive, our men returned to the boats and moved off to a small island about a mile in circumference, where they decided to spend the night. For already a sudden storm at sea had grown so great that it was impossible for them to reach their ships. And then each of the men refreshed himself with a small portion of the victuals that had been placed in the boats for their dinner, for they had had neither food nor drink the day before. Still, they knew not how long the storm would last, how far off the ships might be, or even if they would ever see them again; and so they ate very sparingly. They knew full well that the only nourishment the country could offer them was golden rocks and precious stones—a hard food to live on. And the natives were much more likely to eat them than to give them something to eat. So they posted sentries and lay there the whole night upon cliffs of snow and ice, cold, wet, and comfortless.

While all this was happening to the party on land, the position of the ships at sea was no less perilous. For in less than an hour after the general left in the morning, the *Aid* was set on fire. This was due to the negligence of the cook in overheating the chimney, and of the workman in building it. The fire could very well have destroyed the vessel, but one of the boys happened to see it, and it was quickly extinguished with great effort and God's help. On that same day there were a number of nasty squalls, which by ten o'clock that night grew into a bad storm that continued till morning, putting our ships in serious danger. Surrounded on every side by mountains of ice, we dodged them as well as we could, with some actually scraping against us and others happily missing us by inches. The smallest of those icebergs were as dangerous to strike as any rock and capable of splitting the strongest ship in the world wide open. We found a small patch of clear water—as God willed—to turn in, but otherwise we were surrounded on every side by ice. But the wind was so strong that we could carry only a foresail, and we had so little sea-room that we were forced to tack fourteen times in eight glasses.[5] But with God at the helm, Charles Jackman and Andrew Dyer, the master's mates and both expert mariners, and Richard Cox, the master gunner, managed to avoid most of the dangers with which they were threatened. They were also helped by the very careful sailors they had aboard, and by the fact that the nights were clear and without darkness. These perils seem much more obvious and terrifying in retrospect than they did at the time; for then we had too much to do, using our hands to haul ropes and our eyes to watch for anything that might endanger us.

The next morning, July 21, when the storm ceased, as God willed, the general spotted his ships, brought his captive and his whole company aboard, and told us what had happened on shore. Falling to our knees, we gave humble and hearty thanks that God had been pleased to send us such speedy deliverance from such pressing perils. And so without further ado, we struck over towards the southern shore of the straits.

On July 21 we discovered a deep bay that seemed a likely harbour for our ships. The general rowed there with some of his boats to see if it would, in fact, be a suitable haven, and to search for ore with his goldfiners, as they had not yet assayed anything from the south shore. On the first small island where we landed, all the sands and cliffs were glistening, and they had such a bright marquesset that everything seemed to be made of gold. But when we tested it, it was no better than

[5]That is, in four hours, or one watch.

black lead and verified the proverb: "All is not gold that shineth!"

On July 22 we headed into the sound and anchored a reasonable distance from shore, where we thought we would be safe. But we were immediately threatened by a slab of drift ice which the ebb tide carried out of the sound and cast athwart us before we saw it coming. The men on board heaved mightily at the capstan, overcoming most of the danger by moving the vessel. Yet in spite of their efforts, it struck the stern of the ship such a blow that we were afraid it had knocked off our rudder. This forced us to cut our anchor cable at the hawse and run farther up the sound under a foresail. Fortunately the steerage was stronger than we thought it was at the time or we would have run the ship on the rocks, as there was a very narrow channel to turn in. But with God's help, everything turned out well. We named the place Jackman's Sound after the master's mate who first discovered it. Within the sound was an island that we called Smith's Island (because the blacksmith first set up his forge there), where we found a deposit of silver. It was impossible, however, to get it out of the rocks without a great deal of labour. There our goldfiners assayed the ore that was collected on the north shore and found four different kinds to hold gold in good quantity.

Upon another small island there was also found a large dead fish that had apparently been trapped in the ice. In proportion, it was round like a porpoise, about twelve feet long and of a corresponding bulk, having a horn two yards long growing out of its snout or nostril. The horn is wreathed and straight like a wax taper, and the beast may truly be looked upon as a sea unicorn. Reserved as a jewel by command of the Queen, this horn can be seen in her Wardrop of Robes. Its form is thus:

On Tuesday, July 23, the general landed on the southern mainland, the supposed continent of America, with seventy of his finest gentlemen, soldiers, and sailors. Then, with the sound of a trumpet, he assembled them all around the flag and told them how significant the present work was for the service of Her Majesty, our country, our reputations, and the safety of our own lives. He therefore instructed every man to be orderly, and obedient to those who were placed in command. The leaders he appointed were Captain Fenton, Captain Yorke, and his lieutenant, George Best. Then we formed ourselves into a circle, fell to our knees, and humbly thanked God that it had pleased him in his great goodness to preserve us from such imminent dangers, and to bestow such great and hidden treasures upon us, his poor and unworthy servants. We also besought the assistance of his Holy Spirit in delivering us safely back to our own country, so that the light and truth of our discoveries being known, it might redound to the greater honour of his holy name, and consequently to the advantage of England.

And so, in as good order as the place permitted, we marched towards the tops of the mountains. These were as painful to climb as they were dangerous to descend, because of their steepness and ice. After travelling about five miles by such unwieldy paths, we returned to our ships without seeing any people or any suggestion that the land was inhabited. Several of the gentlemen asked the general if he would permit twenty or thirty of them to march inland for thirty or forty leagues, so that they might explore the land and perform some acceptable service for their country. But the general was not satisfied with the progress that the expedition was making. Knowing that time was running out and that his countrymen had a greedy desire for immediate gains, he bent his entire effort to finding a mine and loading his ships. He was quite content with leaving everything else to be done—with God's help—at some later date.

He therefore returned to the north shore with the two barks on July 26, leaving the *Aid* at anchor in Jackman's Sound. That same night, the barks anchored in a sound where the tide ran so swiftly, and the indraughts of ice were so threatening, that they were seriously endangered. Still, they found a very rich mine and had gathered together almost twenty tons of ore before the ice came drifting into the sound on July 28 to the distress of the barks, which were anchored there. The *Gabriel*, riding astern of the *Michael*, had her cable parted when it was galled by a slab of drifting ice. With this, she lost her third anchor and cable and now had but one left. Although the ice was still pressing into the sound, the vessels were protected from further damage by God's help and by a great iceberg, which fenced them in when it went aground just ahead of them. Had this not happened, I surely think that the ice would have cast them upon the rocks.

The *Michael* fastened herself to the iceberg with her anchor and rode under its lee till about midnight. Then, as the tide went out, the iceberg broke under its own weight close beside the bark, making a sudden and fearful noise. Early the next morning, we weighed anchor with the flood and moved farther up the straits, abandoning in our haste the ore that we had gathered up. We named the place Beare's Sound after the master of the *Michael*, and named the island Leicester's Island.

On one of the small islands in the sound, we found a tomb containing the scattered bones of a man. As the captured native was with us, we asked him by signs if his countrymen had not slain the man to eat his flesh from the bones, so leaving them scattered about. The native denied this, making signs to indicate that the bones had been scattered by wolves or by some other wild beast. On the same island, we also found a large quantity of fish hidden under some stones, and some sleds, bridles, fish-skin kettles, bone knives, and other things belonging to the people of the country. As he was explaining the use of all those things, the native picked up one of the bridles, caught one of our dogs, and harnessed him as we do our horses. Then, sitting on a sled, like one of our coachmen, and picking up a whip, he taught the dog to draw the sled. Thus we saw that they use dogs as we use horses. We found out later that they keep small dogs in their tents as domestic cattle which they fatten up for food. Only the larger sort of dogs is used for drawing sleds.

On July 29, about four leagues from Beare's Sound, we discovered a bay which was fenced in on each side by small islands lying off the mainland. These break the pressure of the tides and keep out most of the drifting ice. We anchored in the lee of a small island in what proved a very fit harbour for our ships. Both the island and the sound are now named after that Right Honourable and virtuous lady, Anne, Countess of Warwick. That is the farthest place we reached within the strait that year, and it is not more than thirty leagues from the cape of the Queen's Foreland at the entrance. On the island where we were anchored was an extensive deposit of ore, in which, when it was washed, gold could be plainly seen. It was therefore thought best to load the ships there, where there was a good supply of reasonably rich ore, rather than run the risk of searching for a better deposit in the little time we had left. So the general put the miners to work. He set a good example by joining them in the mine and showing that he was an energetic workman as well as a good captain. Then every man in the company, both the best and the worst, joined him.

The next day, July 30, the *Michael* was sent over to Jackman's

Sound to fetch the *Aid*. Meanwhile we discovered on the mainland opposite, the poor caves and houses of the country people. These apparently serve as their winter dwellings. They are round like an oven, are built two fathom underground, and are joined together with holes like fox or rabbit warrens. The people undertrench those places with gutters, so that the water falling from the hills above may slide away without annoying them. The houses are usually seated in the foot of a hill for protection from the cold winds, with their doors or entrances always opening towards the south. From the ground upward, they are built of whalebone, because of the scarcity of timber. The whalebones are overlapped and handsomely compacted together at the top, then covered over with seal skins, which are used instead of tiles to keep out the rain. Each house has only one room, with one half of the floor raised a foot higher than the other with flat stones. On this, the inhabitants strew moss and make their nests to sleep in. Defiling their dens most filthily with their beastly feeding, they probably remain in one place until their own sluttishness forces them to seek sweeter air and a new home. They are no doubt a dispersed and wandering people like the Tartars, living in hordes and troops without any certain abode.

At that place our captive, who was ashore with us to explain the use of such things as we saw, stayed behind the rest of us to set up five small sticks in a circle, with a small bone placed right in the middle. When one of our men noticed this, he called us back to look at it, thinking it was a charm or some kind of witchcraft. But it was just a message, so far as we could see, telling his countrymen that he was captured and held a prisoner because they had betrayed and seized five of our men the previous year. He was amazed later when we showed him a picture of his countryman whom we had taken to England on the last voyage. We had had the picture drawn to include a boat and other furniture, and with the native dressed in English clothing as well as his own. Our native looked at the picture for some time in complete silence, trying, no doubt, to decide if he could properly speak to him without straining courtesy; for he seemed to accept the drawing as a living creature. Finally, he began to question him, and became suspicious when he received no answers. With a little help, he would have grown into a rage, but at last, when he handled and felt the picture, he realized it was just a deceptive image. Then he uttered great cries of amazement, for he thought that we could make men live or die at our pleasure.

And now that he was reminded of it, he indicated that he knew that five of our men had been captured the previous year. He numbered the five men on his five fingers, and pointed to one of our boats which was just like the one our men were in when they were lured into captivity. When we made signs suggesting the men had been slain and eaten, he energetically denied it with contrary signs.

On the last day of July, the *Michael* and the *Aid* returned from the south side of the strait to anchor with us in the Countess of Warwick's Sound. They reported that since our departure from Jackman's Sound, nothing of significance had happened until the previous day. Several of the men were visiting a small island that day near the place where the *Aid* was anchored, when they noticed a large boat carrying eighteen or twenty natives. As soon as they saw them, they hurried back to the ship to warn the rest of the crew. From the ship, they watched the natives climb to the top of a hill, where they waved a flag and made a great uproar with noises like so many bulls. Our men fitted out a small skiff with six or seven men and rowed over towards the natives, to see if they might meet together; the skiff was followed by a well-armed, larger boat, so that our men might be rescued if the need arose. But as soon as our men approached them, the natives fled in their boats, either because they were afraid or because they hoped to lure our men farther into their grasp. We followed them, but they paddled away so swiftly that we could not get anywhere near them. We did the best we could, however, and after chasing them more than two miles out to sea, returned to the ships.

The next morning, August 1, Captain Yorke brought the *Michael* into Jackman's Sound and told the *Aid* that he had spent the previous night at anchor in a small bay about four leagues away. He had been carried to leeward of Jackman's Sound by the lack of wind. The place where he spent the night was later named Yorke Sound. He saw some native tents there, so he went ashore with his men to examine them and found that the people had fled, probably out of fear. Among many strange things they found in the tents was the raw and freshly killed flesh of some unknown animal, and some carcasses and bones of dead dogs. They were astonished to find also a doublet of canvas that was made in the English fashion, a shirt, a girdle, and three shoes for contrary feet and of different sizes. Our men were convinced that these were part of the clothing of our five countrymen who had been captured the previous year by the natives about fifty leagues to the west of that place. Hoping that some of the captives might still be alive, the captain left a note telling of our arrival again at Meta Incognita. He also left pen, ink, and paper so that they could send an answer if they should find it. Our men took nothing from the tents and even left some looking-glasses, points, and other toys there as tokens of their friendly intent. Then the captain boarded his vessel and hastened to the *Aid* to tell them what he had found, intending to return to the tents and there, either by force or policy, to entrap or entice the people into a friendly discussion.

When they heard what was afoot, the crew of the *Aid* immediately decided to assist the project. Captain Yorke was joined by the master of the *Aid*, his mate, Charles Jackman, who had been aboard the *Michael* the previous day, and some thirty or forty gentlemen and soldiers. In two small rowing pinnaces, they headed for the place where they had seen the native tents the night before. They put Charles Jackman ashore at a convenient place with a number of men to march overland and surround the natives on one side, while the captain took the rest of the party in the boats to entrap them on the other side. When the boats arrived at the place where the natives had been camped the night before, they found that the tents were gone. Meanwhile, the men who were approaching the camp from the rear were passing over two or three tedious mountains when they happened to notice some tents in a valley below. They were near a creek beside the sea, and because they were in a different place from the ones seen the night before, our men thought it was a different group. They started to encircle the tents, determined to capture the natives if possible, but were quickly spotted. Launching two boats, a large one and a small one, about sixteen or eighteen of the people put out to sea after a narrow escape. Our soldiers who were following them along the shore discharged their calivers, hoping that the noise would be heard by the men in our boats. And indeed, the boats were just then crossing the mouth of the sound. Their presence blocked off the channel, preventing the native boats from getting sea-room, where we would never have overtaken them by rowing, and forcing them ashore on a point of land within the sound. That point has since been named Bloody Point because of the slaughter that occurred there that day. Our men followed so swiftly behind them that the natives had little time in which to attempt an escape.

As soon as they landed, each native broke his paddle, hoping thus to prevent us from carrying away their boats. Then they turned desperately upon our men, resisting them manfully during their landing, and so long as they still had arrows and darts. Even the arrows that were shot at them by our men were picked up and fired back, and some were even plucked from their bodies before they were

Eskimo, by John White. White's paintings are the first
pictures of Eskimo ever made.

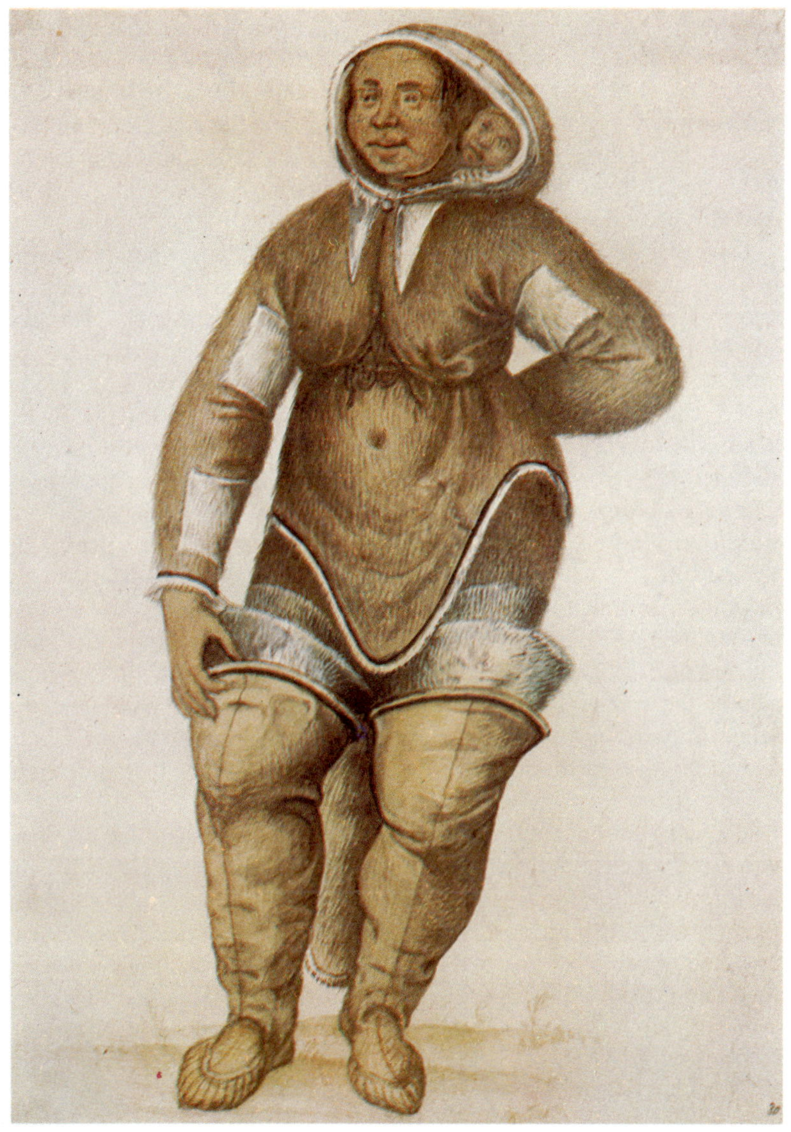

Eskimo woman and child, by John White

returned. Thus they maintained their cause until both weapons and life utterly failed them. And when they found that they were mortally wounded—and being ignorant of the meaning of mercy—they cast themselves with deadly fury off the rocks into the sea. Perhaps they feared that their enemies might receive some honour through their dead carcasses or might even eat them, for they thought we were probably cannibals.

During the conflict, one of our men was seriously wounded in the belly by an arrow, and five or six of the natives were slain. Except for two women, the rest of the natives escaped among the rocks. Because one of the women was old and ugly, our men let her go, thinking she must be a devil or a witch. The other woman was young, and encumbered with a nursing child at her back, so she hid among the rocks, where she was found by one of our men. Thinking she was a man, he shot her; the arrow went through her hair and pierced the child's arm. Our surgeon applied salves to the wound, but she was not acquainted with that kind of surgery so she removed our medicine from the wound and applied her own remedy. She healed the child's arm by licking it continually with her own tongue, which was not unlike that of our dogs. And then because the day was almost over, the men hurried back to join those who had remained at the tents on the other side of the sound. There they found the clothing, the letter, and the other English furniture which had been in the camp that Captain Yorke discovered the night before, and which told us that they were the same people.

When we considered the sudden flight of the natives and the desperation with which they fought, we began to doubt that we would ever again see the five men whom they had captured the previous year. Because their disposition is so ravenous and bloody that they will eat any kind of raw flesh or carrion, no matter how rotten, it is very likely that they killed and devoured our men. And the doublet which we found in one of their tents was full of holes that had been made with their arrows or darts.

Then, as night was falling, the men rounded up their captives and such poor stuff as was found in the tents, and returned to their ships. On the way they were struck by a sudden squall, which the small boats found quite dangerous, but, as God willed, they all arrived safely. Then, as was mentioned earlier, they returned with their good news to the Countess of Warwick's Sound.

It is at least nine leagues from Jackman's Sound to the Countess of Warwick's Sound, across the narrowest part of the strait. These sounds lie directly opposite each other, with Jackman's being on the south side, some thirty leagues from the Queen's Foreland which stands at the south side of the entrance to the straits. This cape lies to the north of the New Found Land, and on the same continent of America, for anything that is known to the contrary.

Now that we had a native woman for the comfort of the man we had captured earlier, we brought them both together, with our men watching silently to observe the nature of their meeting. At first they looked at each other wistfully, and for a long time, without uttering a sound, but with lively changes in their colouring and expressions. It seemed as though the grief and shame of their captivity had deprived them of the use of their tongues. Suddenly the woman turned away and began to sing. It was as if she did not see the man, disdained to notice him, or was preoccupied with some other matter. The next time they were brought together, the man broke the silence first. With stern and solemn countenance he began to tell the woman a long, serious tale; she listened attentively and without interruption till it was finished. Later on, when they were better acquainted, I doubt that either one would have survived without the comfort of the other. And although they lived together continually, as near as we could see they never used each other as man and wife, even though the woman did everything that would be expected of a good housewife. She kept their cabin clean—and him when he was seasick—killed and flayed the dogs that they ate, and prepared his meals. And all the while they were so modest that the man would never change his clothes without first sending the woman out of his cabin. They were also most careful that their private parts were not exposed to each other or to anyone else.

On Monday, August 6, the lieutenant went ashore with the soldiers, forty in all, to protect the miners who were working on the Countess of Warwick's Island. After pitching their tents, they fortified the place as well as they could. Then, when they were all at work, they noticed a number of natives on the top of a hill opposite them on the mainland. They were waving a flag, uttering loud cries, and seemed to be the same people that our men had recently met on the south shore. They had come to complain of their late losses and to beg for the restitution of the woman and child whom our men had captured. The general sent the woman to the highest point on the island so that she could easily be seen; then, taking the man with him, he went to confer with the natives. When our captive first met his friends face to face, he was so overwhelmed with tears that for a long time he could not speak a word. But overcoming his compassion, finally, he talked freely with his friends and gave them such toys and trifles as he had received from us. We noticed that they are very kind to one another and grieve deeply for the loss of their friends. Using signs, our general demanded the return of the five men whom they had captured the previous year. In return, he promised to release the prisoners we had taken and to reward them also with great gifts and friendship. After talking with his friends, our native made signs suggesting that the five men were still alive and would be returned. They suggested, too, that we should write letters to our men; for they knew very well what use we make of writing. This knowledge they had either from our poor countrymen whom they had captured, or from our own captive who had seen us writing and then repeating such words in his language as we wished to learn. Because it was late, however, they had to leave without any letter, even though they called for one most earnestly. Early the next morning, August 7, they again called for the letter. When we gave it to them, they hastily departed, holding up three fingers and pointing at the sun to indicate that they meant to return in three days. We heard nothing more from them till the appointed time, when they returned in a manner that I will tell you about later.

That night, because the natives were very close, the lieutenant had the trumpeter assemble all the men on the island. Gathering them around the flag, he reminded them of how far they were from their native land, and of the number of people who threatened them if a sharp lookout was not kept. For at low water the enemy might almost cross from the mainland to the island on foot. He therefore urged the men to be prepared for every eventuality, gave them the watchword, and went to bed.

I thought that the captain's letter was well worth recording, not only for the curious circumstances in which it was written, but for its substance. I therefore repeat it here, just as it was hastily written:

In the name of God, in whom we all believe, who I trust hath preserved your bodies and souls amongst these infidels, I commend me unto you. I will be glad to seek by all means you can devise for your deliverance, either with force, or with any commodities within my ships, which I will not spare for your sakes, or anything else I can do for you. I have aboard, of theirs, a man, a woman, and a child, which I am contented to deliver for you, but the man which I carried away from hence the last year is dead in England. Moreover, you may declare unto them, that if they deliver you not, I will not leave a man alive in their country. And thus, if one of you can come to speak with

A skirmish with the Eskimo, by John White

me, they shall have either the man, the woman, or child in pawn for
you. And thus unto God, whom I trust you do serve, in haste I leave
you, and to him we will daily pray for you. This Tuesday morning the
seventh of August, Anno. 1577.

Yours to the uttermost of my power,
Martin Frobisher

Postscript: I have sent you by these bearers, pen, ink, and paper, to
write back unto me again, if personally you can not come to certify me
of your estate.

By now, the general had changed his mind about going farther into
the straits at that time to continue his exploration. He had already
captured a man and a woman, which he thought was sufficient for
learning the language. And he had already met with the people who
had captured our men last year, as we learned from the English furniture which we found in their tents, so that there was no reason to look
for them farther off. In addition, it was so late in the season that he
thought it best to bend all his efforts towards gathering up ore, and to
leave any further exploration for some other time. For his commission
instructed him to search only for the golden ore, and to put off all
further search for the northwest passage.

On Thursday, August 9, we started to build a small fort for our
defence on the Countess of Warwick's Island. We entrenched ourselves on the corner of a cliff which was surrounded and well fenced
by the sea on three sides, like a wall of good height. We finished the
other side with cakes of earth to good purpose and named the fort
Best's Bulwark after the lieutenant who built it. We fortified the place
because we were afraid that the natives might overwhelm us with their
numbers, rather than through any fear we had of their power, weapons,
or tactics. And wisdom would suggest that we should not be too care-
less when we were so far from home. In addition, we were alarmed by
the signs that our captive made regarding the arrival of his governor
or prince, whom he called Catchoe. He showed us that this Catchoe
was a much bigger man than any of us, and that he was accustomed
to being carried on the shoulders of his men. About midnight, therefore, the lieutenant raised a false alarm on the island to see how well
prepared the men were. He also wanted to see what assistance the
ships would be able to provide on short notice, if the need arose. He
found that everyone was prepared for a sudden attack.

On Saturday, August 11, the native people again appeared, calling to us from the side of a hill on the opposite shore. Hoping to hear of his men, and perhaps even to find an answer to his letter, the general crossed over to meet them. No more than three of the natives were visible, but a great many more were hidden among the rocks. They hoped to capture some of us, in order to redeem their own, by leading our boat around a point of land and out of sight of the rest of our company, but our men were suspicious and would not be drawn into the trap. One of our men was put ashore, where he picked up a large bladder which one of the natives offered us, left a looking-glass in its place, then returned to the boat. In the meantime, some of the men were stationed on the Countess of Warwick's Island, where they might look down on the others and see things that might not be visible from the boat. Suddenly they yelled, having seen a number of the natives creeping behind the rocks towards our men. So the general left without any news of the men who were captives.

Our native said that the bladder we received in trade was really a gift for him and was to keep drinking-water in. We suspected, however, that it was sent to him so that he could escape by swimming, for both he and the woman had already tried to escape several times in our boats. They had untied them from the stern of our ships, hoping to escape with all of them so that we could not pursue them. Fortunately, they were spotted in time.

After the general left, twenty of the natives lined up in plain sight on the top of a hill, holding their hands over their heads and dancing and singing with great gusto. We thought they put on the display so that we could see how strong they were and be tempted, perhaps, to display our own strength. They continued dancing upon the hilltop until we fired a piece of our great ordnance that night. Thundering through the valleys, this made such a fearful noise that they decided to leave. We fired the gun as a display of force rather than to do them any harm.

On Sunday, August 12, Captain Fenton mustered the soldiers and had them skirmish among themselves. This not only provided exercise for the men, it also showed the country people that we were always on our guard, for almost certainly the natives were hidden in the surrounding hills, watching our every move.

On Wednesday, August 14,[6] the general took two small, well-armed boats into a bay within the sound to search for ore, and again

[6]Comparison with the date mentioned in the previous paragraph shows that Best's chronology is confused at this point.

he met the country people whom he suspected of lurking about. As soon as they saw our men, they made a great noise and waved a white flag made of bladders sewn together with the guts and sinews of beasts. They waved us towards them, showing no more than three of their number. But when we approached them, we could see a great multitude of them creeping among the rocks, so that we were convinced of their treachery. We indicated that if they would lay aside their arms and come forth, we would treat them as friends, although their own intent was manifest to us. In spite of all the signs of friendship we could make, they still came creeping towards us through the rocks, hoping to take advantage of us. They seemed to think that we had no eyes to see them, or that our simple wits could not see through such obvious devices as theirs. Their spokesman invited us with many enticing motions to come ashore to eat and sleep, and tried to persuade us with a great show of courtesy, clapping his bare hands over his head as a sign of peace and innocence. To influence our hungry stomachs he brought us a fine bait of raw meat, which we plucked aboard with a boat-hook so as not to offend him. But when the cunning Catchoe saw that his cold morsel failed to sharpen our appetites, he cast about for a serving of warm flesh. He had one of his men come limping from behind the rocks as though he were lame. Then, hoisting the lame man upon his shoulders, he carried him to the water's edge and left him there, to be taken by us at our leisure. He hoped that we would bite at his bait and leap ashore, so that they could apprehend some of us to use as ransom for the captives we had taken. But I suspect that our flesh is such sweet meat for them that if they ever got their hands on us they would hardly part with such tasty morsels. The gentlemen and soldiers were very anxious to go ashore and attack them, but the general was more cautious and hoped to pacify them gradually rather than make spoil of them. He therefore refused to allow any person to expose himself to the danger of going ashore, as he was interested only in collecting ore at the moment, and not in conquest.

However, to test the footmanship of the "cripple", he permitted one of the men to shoot at him. Receiving a parting blow, the "cripple" darted behind a rock, and when he left he was a true cripple rather than a feigned one. Then his companions, who had been hidden among the rocks, suddenly came forward to continue the skirmish with their slings, bows, and arrows, dashing fiercely to the very edge of the water. They followed us along the coast in complete desperation, and totally without fear of our arrows or anything else. Their own arrows, meanwhile, all fell short of us and were of little consequence. These natives had been lying in wait for us all along the coast and, being spread out like that, were not easy to count, but we could see over 100 of them and had reason to suspect that a greater number were present. And so, without loss or injury, we returned again to our ships.

By this time, our task was coming to an end. With only five poor miners and the help of a few gentlemen and soldiers, we had carried aboard almost 200 tons of gold ore in twenty days. All the men were pleased with what they had done and were determined to work lustily to bring our labours to a swift and happy conclusion.

On Wednesday night, August 21, we finally finished the job. And it was indeed time to leave, for the men were weary, their shoes and clothes were in tatters, the bottoms had been torn out of their baskets, and all their tools were broken. Some of the men, too, were seriously injured through straining themselves: some were ruptured, and others made lame. About that time, ice began to form around the ships at night, warning us that the sun was moving south and that we must hurry homeward.

It should be noted—and remembered to their credit—that the gentlemen and soldiers on this voyage left all thought of reputation aside. With great willingness and courage, they overcame most of the difficulties of a monumental task in a very short time. The ore they brought home bears witness that this be true, without any further proof. May God grant that they be as well thought of as their honest merit deserves.

We plucked down our tents on Thursday, August 22, built bonfires upon the top of the highest hill, and marched around the island with the flag flying. We fired a farewell volley of shot in honour of the Right Honourable Lady Anne, Countess of Warwick, for whom the island was named, and so departed.

On August 23, having a good west wind, we sailed for home; but the wind soon dropped, forcing us to anchor just inside the entrance to the sound. When the wind returned about three o'clock the next morning, we again set sail, and by nine that night the Queen's Foreland had dropped astern, and we were clear of the straits and were pushing out into the broad Atlantic. We shaped our course somewhat to the south, so that we would soon be under the latitude of our home port. The wind was very great at sea that night, so we lay a-hull while the snow piled up half a foot thick on the hatches. From the twenty-fourth to the twenty-eighth it continued very windy, but as it was a favourable wind, we held our course south-southeast; we got separated from the barks, but by good fortune we met them again. On August 29 there was such a strong northeast wind that we could carry only a bunt of our foresail, and the barks could carry no sail at all. We got separated from the *Michael* and suspected that she would head for the Orkneys, for that was the way they knew best.

On August 30 both the master and the boatswain of the *Gabriel* were washed overboard in a high wind and raging sea, in spite of the fact that the vessel was laced fore and aft with breast-high ropes. The boatswain was fortunately saved when he grabbed a rope that was hanging overboard, but the master, William Smith, was drowned. Although he was still a young man, he was a skilled mariner. He had been in a very good mood the previous morning, when he had told the captain of a dream in which he was washed overboard and could not be saved, even though the boatswain grabbed him by the hand. And indeed his dream came true. For when they were in fact washed overboard, the boatswain grabbed a rope with one hand and the master with the other, but his strength failed and the master was drowned.

At that point, we reckoned we were 200 leagues from the Queen's Foreland on our homeward voyage. On the last day of August, about midnight, we had two or three sudden gusts of wind.

By September 1 the storm had grown very bad, continuing all day and most of the night. As we drifted under bare poles to wait for the barks, the ship was pounded heavily by the seas; we were in such danger of being pooped that we tried to ease the rolling of the ship with the bunt of a sail. The *Gabriel* was not able to keep up with us then because she had to continue lying a-hull, and because we drifted much faster in any event, being a tall ship with a higher poop to catch the wind. Finally we could see them no more, so we left them to God and the western sea. On the morning of September 2, when it pleased God to end the storm, we noticed that the rudder of the ship was split and almost ready to fall off. Taking advantage of the calm sea, we flung a dozen of our best men overboard to repair it. Working very carefully under water, they mended and strengthened the rudder with planks, which they lashed on with ropes. Most of the men were more than half dead when we plucked them out of the water, but it was God's pleasure that the sea remained calm till the work was finished.

During the voyage we usually determined our latitude by measuring the height of the sun, because the long polar day makes it impossible to see Polaris or the other fixed stars. And in that region the North Star is elevated so high above the horizon that it cannot be measured accurately with the cross-staff, and the degrees marked on the astrolabe are too small to measure minutes. Therefore we always used the cross-staff and the sun, as the fittest instruments for this purpose.

We spent the next four or five days beating our way southward against contrary winds, trying to reach the latitude of Scilly. Then on September 11, about six o'clock at night, the wind shifted to the southwest, and we set our course southeast. By Thursday, September 12, we reckoned we were not more than 150 leagues from Scilly; the weather was fair, and the wind was on our starboard quarter as we continued our course to the southeast. When we checked our position on the thirteenth, we were at the same latitude as Scilly and about twelve leagues off, so we headed due east towards the sleeve or channel. On Sunday, September 15, about four o'clock in the afternoon, we went on soundings in fifty-one fathom with a bottom of fine white sand. We reckoned from this that we were on the back of Scilly, so we set our course east by north, then slowly shifted it to east-northeast, and finally northeast.

About eight o'clock in the morning on September 16, soundings showed that we were in sixty-five fathom with a bottom of sandy ooze, which suggested that we were athwart St. George's Channel, just over the edge of the banks. That night, carrying only a small sail, we took many soundings, all of which showed about forty fathom, which was so shallow we could not tell where we were. The next day we were still in forty fathom, but the sandy bottom with small worms and cockle-shells showed that we were not far off Land's End. So we slipped through between Scilly and Land's End. We were now in the bay, but were still not able to double about a point on a south by east course. With the wind at the southwest by west, we were forced to come about, but could still not double the point to get clear of Land's End and beat up the channel. Then the weather cleared when we were hard aboard the shore, and we just cleared Land's End to head up St. George's Channel.

Because the weather was very foul at sea, and because our steerage was damaged, we coveted the protection of a harbour, so we anchored in Padstow Road in Cornwall. But riding there in the roadstead was very dangerous, and we were advised by the local people to put to sea again, and of two evils to choose the lesser, for there was nothing but peril where we were. So we plied along the channel to Lundy, but this too was an open road, and, in addition, our anchor would not hold. Again the weather forced us to put to sea. Finally, about September 23, we arrived at Milford Haven, a very good harbour in Wales. We were very pleased to know that at last we had arrived safely; and we were equally pleased to know that with our arrival our country and commonwealth would be enriched with the knowledge of our discovery.

About a month after we arrived at Milford Haven, the Lords of the Council ordered us to take the ship to Bristol and to deposit the ore in the castle there for safe-keeping. When we got there, we found that the *Gabriel* had arrived ahead of us in perfect safety. After the master was lost, there was no one on board who could bring her home; but by good fortune she met a ship from Bristol just as she approached the coast, and the ship guided her safely into port.

At Bristol we also heard the good news that our other bark, the *Michael*, had arrived safely in one of the northern ports. Thus did it please God to bring us all together again.

We lost but a single person during the entire voyage, apart from one man who died at sea; and he was sick when he came aboard. But he was so anxious to join the expedition that he chose to die in the attempt rather than be excluded from so notable a voyage.

End of the Second Voyage.

1578

The Third Frobisher Voyage

The stones of this supposed continent with
America, be altogether sparkled, and glitter
in the sun like gold.

Dionyse Settle, 1577

1578

The Third Frobisher Voyage

The
THIRD VOYAGE OF CAPTAIN FROBISHER,
pretended for the discovery of Cathay,
by Meta Incognita
ANNO DO. 1578

Having returned from the second voyage, the general repaired immediately to the Court at Windsor to advise Her Majesty of the success and prosperity of his voyage, the abundance of gold ore he had found, and of other things of importance that he had discovered in those northern parts. He was heartily welcomed and courteously entertained by many noblemen, but was especially commended by Her Majesty for his great adventure. Her Majesty also praised the rest of the gentlemen of the expedition for the great energy with which they carried out such an exhausting and dangerous enterprise. She commented very favourably upon the good order that had been maintained, and upon the readiness of the men in carrying out their various professional duties and in doing whatever else the general should command. Her Majesty's gracious commendation encouraged the officers and gentlemen so much that they spared neither hardship, limb, nor life in bringing the matter to a happy and prosperous conclusion, and thus in confirming Her Majesty's good and honourable opinion of them.

Because the gold ore portended great profit and riches, and because the voyage itself increased greatly the hope of finding a northwest passage to Cathay, Her Majesty appointed special commissioners, chosen for their judgement, art, and skill, to examine all aspects of the matter and to deal with everything pertaining to the project. And because the place and country where Frobisher had been had never before been discovered, and therefore had no name by which it might be called, Her Majesty very properly called it Meta Incognita. After assaying the ore, and weighing the sundry reasons and substantial grounds for believing that a northwest passage might be found that way, the commissioners advised Her Highness that the matter was one of great importance and that another voyage was worthy of royal support. So preparations were immediately made to assemble the ships, as well as all the other things that would be required. And because it was already late in the year, plans for the voyage had to be pushed forward expeditiously. It was assumed that gold from the mines that had already been discovered would more than defray the entire costs of the expedition. To protect the mines and lands that had already been discovered, and to carry out further exploration—particularly in the interior, to see what secrets might be hidden there—it was decided that a number of chosen soldiers and discreet men should be left there to establish a settlement in Meta Incognita. This group would also continue the search for the passage to Cathay, as the hope of finding such a passage was increasing daily. To house the men who were to remain in Meta Incognita, a strong fort or house was cunningly devised and artfully framed of timber by a notable learned man. It was to be carried there by ship, and would protect the men not only from the dangers of falling snow and cold air, but also from the natives, who might otherwise overwhelm them.

Many forward-looking gentlemen volunteered to join this great adventure and noble undertaking. Foremost among them was Captain Fenton, lieutenant general for Captain Frobisher, who shared the command with him. The day-to-day management of the operation was left largely to the discretion of Captain Best and Captain Filpot. Because they placed the common good of the country above their personal safety, they were willing to remain in Meta Incognita. They were prepared to expose themselves to the hazards of living among a savage and brutish people in a place that was always thought to be uninhabitable because of the extreme cold.

One hundred of the men had volunteered to remain the whole year in Meta Incognita and had been accepted: of these, forty were sailors and would man the three ships that were to winter there; thirty were miners who would gather together the gold ore for shipment home the next year; and thirty were soldiers for the protection of the others. This last group included the gentlemen, goldfiners, bakers, carpenters, and other necessary tradesmen. To each of the captains—that is, to the men in charge of the soldiers, sailors, and miners—was assigned one ship, which was to be used both for further exploration of the country and for bringing the men back to England if the fleet failed to arrive the following year, or if anything should happen which could make it necessary to return earlier.

When everything was prepared, there were fifteen good ships ready to set sail. Of these, twelve were to return, laden with gold ore, at the end of the summer, while the other three would be left with the men who were to remain there. And then, when all arrangements were completed, the general, with all the captains, repaired to the Court at Greenwich to take their leave of Her Majesty. She graciously encouraged them all and, besides other gifts and greater promises, gave the general a fair chain of gold: then the captains kissed her hand, took their leave, and each returned to his ship.

THE SHIPS AND THEIR CAPTAINS

1.	The *Aid*	Captain Frobisher
2.	The *Thomas Allen*	Captain Yorke
3.	The *Judith*	Captain Fenton
4.	The *Anne Frances*	Captain Best
5.	The *Hopewell*	Captain Carew
6.	The *Bear*	Captain Filpot
7.	The *Thomas of Ipswich*	Captain Tanfield
8.	The *Emanuel of Exeter*	Captain Courtney
9.	The *Frances of Foy*	Captain Moyles
10.	The *Moon*	Captain Upcot
11.	The *Ema. of Bridgewater*	Captain Newton
12.	*The Salmon of Weymouth*	Captain Randal
13.	The *Dennis*	Captain Kendall
14.	The *Gabriel*	Captain Harvey
15.	The *Michael*	Captain Kinnersley

On May 27, 1578, these fifteen ships arrived at Harwich, where the general and the other captains mustered and reviewed their companies. Then the general gave each captain a copy of the following orders:

Articles and orders to be observed by the Fleet, to keep the ships together and on course. Set down by Captain Frobisher, General, and delivered in writing to every captain on May 31.

1. First, to banish swearing, dice, card playing, and filthy communication; and to serve God twice a day with the ordinary service of the Church of England, and to clear the glass according to the old order in England.

2. The admiral shall carry a light, and after his light is displayed, no man is to go ahead of him, but is to set his sails so as to follow as closely as possible without endangering anyone else.

3. No man, either by day or night, shall depart more than one English mile from the admiral. Each ship shall stay as close as possible to the admiral without endangering any other ship.

4. If the wind shifts in thick weather, forcing the admiral to come about either by day or by night, he shall give warning by firing a cannon before coming about. This warning shall be answered by both the vice-admiral and the rear-admiral firing a cannon if it is at night or in a fog, and with the vice-admiral answering first and the rear-admiral last.

5. No man in the fleet shall on any occasion give chase to any strange ship or ships that may be encountered, unless he has first spoken with the admiral.

6. Every evening, each ship shall move up and speak with the admiral at seven o'clock, or between seven and eight. If the weather will not permit them all to speak with the admiral, then some of them shall speak with the vice-admiral and receive their instructions from Mr. Hall, chief pilot of the fleet.

7. If an accident should happen to any ship in the fleet, it shall immediately fire two shots of a cannon, and if the accident happens at night, the ship shall show two lights as well.

8. If any ship in the fleet overtakes another ship at night and does not know which ship it is, he shall use this watchword: "Before the world was God." If the other ship is a member of our fleet, he shall answer: "After God, came Christ, his Son." Thus if any ship be found amongst us that is not of our company, he that first discovers him shall warn the admiral himself, or else send another if there is one near him that is a faster vessel.

9. When it is foggy, which usually happens when there is very little wind, each ship in the fleet shall keep up a reasonable noise with trumpet, drum, or some similar device, so that they can keep themselves clear of one another.

10. If the admiral lies a-hull in thick or misty weather, he will first give warning by firing a cannon and putting up three lights one above another, so that every ship may take in its sails; he will give the same signal if he sets sail again before it is clear.

11. If any ship should discover land at night, it will give the same signal that is used for an accident; by night it shall show two lights and fire two shots, and by day it shall fire one shot, fly all its flags, and strike all its sails.

12. If any ship or ships shall get separated from the others in bad weather, they shall sail to Friesland and then continue to the straits. After arriving there, all such ships shall fire a cannon every watch, and keep a sharp lookout for smoke, and for the fire which those that arrive first shall start every night until the entire fleet is assembled.

13. At the sight of an ensign at the masthead of the admiral and the sound of a cannon-shot, each ship shall repair to the admiral to confer with the general.

14. If any enemy is encountered, four ships shall attend upon the admiral, viz. the *Frances of Foy*, the *Moon*, the *Dennis*, and the *Gabriel*; four upon the lieutenant general in the *Judith*, viz. the *Hopewell*, the *Ema.*, the *Bear*, and the *Salmon*; and the other four upon the vice-admiral, viz. the *Anne Frances*, the *Thomas of Ipswich*, the *Emanuel*, and the *Michael*.

15. If there should happen to be any disordered person in the fleet, he is to be taken and kept in safe custody until he may conveniently be brought aboard the admiral, where he will receive such punishment as his offences shall deserve.

By me Martin Frobisher.

Our Departure from England

Having received these articles and orders, we departed from Harwich on May 31, and, sailing along the south coast of England, we came at length to the coast of Ireland at Cape Clear on June 6. There we gave chase to a small bark which we supposed to be a pirate or rover-of-the-sea, but which turned out, in fact, to be some poor men of Bristol. They had met with a company of Frenchmen, who had spoiled and slain many of them and left the rest so sorely wounded that they seemed likely to perish in the sea, having no way of helping themselves nor victuals to sustain their hungry bodies. But our general understood the duties of a soldier and an Englishman, as well as the law of the sea. He took pity on the miseries of the poor men, and sustained them with surgery and salves to heal their wounds, and with meat and drink to comfort their pining hearts. Some of the men reported that they had had nothing to eat or drink for several days but olives and stinking water.

After this good deed, we continued our voyage before a favourable wind without stopping to take on fresh water or any of the provisions that many vessels were short of. Sailing northward along the west coast of Ireland, we met with a great current sweeping out of the southwest; according to our reckoning, it carried us one point to the northeastward of our course and seemed to continue towards Norway and the other northeast parts of the world. We believe that this is the same current that the Portuguese meet at the Cape of Good Hope. From there it strikes over to the Straits of Magellan, is blocked by the narrowness of the straits, and runs into the great Bay of Mexico, where it also meets an obstruction and is forced back again to the northeast as we find it here. We found it farther to the northwards, also, as shall presently be explained more fully.

We sailed on for about two weeks without seeing any land or any living thing except some birds such as wylmots, nodies, gulls, etc., which seem to live entirely at sea in those parts. Then on June 20, at two o'clock in the morning, the general sighted land, which he found to be West Friesland (now named West England). Here the general and some other gentlemen went ashore; as near as we know, they were the first Christians ever to set foot on that ground. The general therefore took possession of the land to the use of our Sovereign Lady, the Queen's Majesty. He discovered there a good harbour for the ships and noticed several little native boats. After he landed, his men saw several tents and some of the natives themselves, and after examining the clothing and other things which they found in the tents, they decided that these people were very much like those of Meta Incognita. As soon as they saw our men coming towards them, these savage and simple people fled fearfully away, supposing there had been no other world than theirs. They seemed to be greatly amazed at such a strange sight as creatures of human shape, yet so different from themselves in clothing, complexion, and other things. In their haste they left all their furniture and other things behind them in their tents, where we found a box of nails, well-cut boards of fir, and several other things that were artfully fashioned. This would indicate that the natives either trade with some civil people or are themselves very skilled workmen. Our men brought away with them only two dogs, which they paid for by leaving behind a number of bells, looking-glasses, and toys.

That country would no doubt provide great trade and riches if it were thoroughly explored. Some of the men thought that West England was connected with the northeast part of Meta Incognita or else with Greenland, because the people, their clothing, their boats, etc. are so much alike. Another reason for this belief is the great number of islands of ice that are found between West England and Meta Incognita. These would argue the presence of a bay lying to the north, and this could only be if the two lands were joined.

On June 23 we set sail for Frobisher's Straits before a fair and favourable wind. The last thing that we saw in West England was a high cliff, and because of a certain similarity, we named it Charing Cross; then we headed south towards the open sea, because to the north we had met with much drifting ice, and this would have been troublesome in fog or thick weather. On Monday, the last day of June, we encountered large whales that were as plentiful as porpoises. In fact, the *Salmon* ran into one of the whales when she was under both her courses and bonnets. She struck the whale squarely, and so solidly that the ship was stopped dead in her tracks, while the whale made a great and ugly noise, arched his body and tail, and dived. Two days later we found a large dead whale floating on the surface, which was probably the same one that was struck by the *Salmon*.

We sighted the Queen's Foreland on July 2, early in the morning, and stood in towards the land all day. Passing through great quantities of drifting ice, we finally entered the strait, only to find that our way was completely blocked. The strait was frozen solid from one side to the other, with walls, mountains, and bulwarks of ice choking up the passage and denying us entrance. And yet I do not think that this passage, or the sea in this area generally, is frozen over at any time of the year, even though it appeared to be because of the great quantity of ice that was occupying the whole straits. I think, rather, that this ice is bred in the hollow sounds and streams, loosened by the heat of the summer sun, then carried out into the strait by the ebb tide, and so is gathered there in such great abundance.

I would like to comment here on the ancient opinion that the Frozen Sea lies in these parts. I think that the whole thing is nothing but conjecture and that no one has ever had personal experience with any such sea. When people speak of the Frozen Sea, we may truly think that they are talking about this region. For this may indeed be called the icy sea. But it may not be called the Frozen Sea, for no sea consisting of salt water can be frozen, as I have demonstrated in my second book. For it seems impossible for any tidal water to freeze, especially if the tidal range is above ten fathom. And also, those islands of ice which we sometimes meet 100 miles from land taste fresh when you gather them out of the salt sea and, when melted, become sweet and wholesome water.

We may have encountered more ice this year than we did on earlier voyages because the winds from the east and south brought us to Meta Incognita sooner than we expected. The same wind, blowing directly into the strait, also prevented the ice from being carried by the ebb tide out to sea, where it would have melted more rapidly. This floating ice is dangerous, because it is packed so tightly together that a man may walk ten or twelve miles over the frozen surface as easily as if it were one piece of ice. It is dangerous, too, because of the way that the tides and swells will suddenly open broad leads and then, with equal suddenness, close them again. Thus it sometimes happens that one ship will be following another under full sail when the lead will close so suddenly that the second ship is trapped. Many times our ships were seriously endangered in this way because they could not take in their sails quickly enough or be brought to a sufficiently sudden stop.

On many occasions we were forced to stem and strike such great chunks of ice that we seemed to be threading our way through mountains. By this means, some of the ships forced their way so far into the ice, in their eagerness to reach port, that it is a great wonder they escaped or were ever heard of again. As it was, we were already missing two of the ships, the *Judith*, with the lieutenant general, Captain Fenton aboard, and the *Michael*, both of which we thought were lost, as we had neither seen nor heard of them for more than twenty days.

One of our ships, the *Dennis*, of 100 tons burden, was actually sunk during this time. She was trying to pick her way through the ice when she received such a blow from one of the pieces that she went down in sight of the whole fleet. However, having warned the others of her distress by firing one of her great guns, the other ships came so quickly to her assistance that the men were all taken off in boats. But part of the house that was to be erected in Meta Incognita for the men who were to spend the winter there went down with the ship.

This was a most fearful spectacle for the fleet to behold, for the outrageous storm which presently followed threatened them all with a similar fate. For the fleet now found itself completely surrounded with ice: behind them were the thick fields of ice through which they had just passed; and before them a totally impenetrable mass. And then they were struck by a sudden and terrible tempest. Sweeping directly into the straits from the southeast, it piled up all the drifting ice behind them and thus barred them from turning back to gain sea-room. When they found themselves surrounded in this way by danger on every side, the men tried to save themselves in a variety of ways. Some of the ships, finding a small berth of sea-room, a place relatively clear of ice, took in their sails and simply lay there adrift. Others moored themselves to a great island of ice and rode under its lee, thinking it would offer them at least some protection from the outrageous winds and the smaller pieces of floating ice. And some were trapped so tightly, and were surrounded by such an infinite number of gigantic slabs of ice, that they were forced to submit both themselves and their ships to the mercy of that unmerciful ice. All they could do was strengthen the sides of their ships with pieces of old cables, beds, masts, planks, and similar things, which they hung overboard to help protect themselves from the outrageous pressure and blows of the ice.

As it is easiest to discover outstanding men in times of great distress, so it is worth noting the invincible spirit with which every captain encouraged his company. The incredible labour with which the sailors and the miners, who were unacquainted with such extremities, overcame the threat of such great and terrible dangers, to the everlasting renown of our nation, should be noted too. Some of the men had even gone over the sides of the ships to stand and work on the ice itself, while others helped them from the deck. Together, they used poles, pikes, pieces of timber, and oars to fend off the ice. Without any rest, they worked day and night exposed to such incredible pain and peril that it was wonderful to behold. Had they not fended off the ice in this fashion, it would almost certainly have pierced the sides of their ships in spite of their former provisions. For rising and falling with the swell of the sea, the huge blocks of ice were seen to slice through planks that were more than three inches thick. They did this, too, with incredible ease. In addition, it was reported by many substantial witnesses that our ships, even the largest and most heavily laden, were sometimes pinched between islands of ice so hard that they were raised up out of the sea more than a foot and had their knees and timbers both bent and broken.

In the midst of these extremities, while some of the men were labouring to save the ships and their own lives, others, through prayer and meditation, were trying to save their souls. For they were sure that their deliverance would be impossible without miraculous intervention. Although there were none who were idle, the ones who felt most secure had nothing to protect them—God knows—but unsupported hope. Except for four ships, the whole fleet, with all the miserable men, remained there the whole night and part of the next day, distressed with their extremities and without any hope of escaping. The four ships which did escape, the *Anne Frances*, the *Moon*, the *Frances of Foy*, and the *Gabriel*, were not quite so far into the strait as the rest of the fleet, and thus were not so securely held by the ice. Being fast ships, and therefore more manoeuvrable than the others, they tried to ride out the storm under sail, though they were barely able to carry a single course each. And because the sea was covered with floating ice, they were in extreme peril many times from mountains of ice that they escaped only by inches. Had they struck those mountains of ice, they would surely have been destroyed, because of the speed with which they were travelling and the unwieldiness of the ships. Still, they thought they would be safer, under the circumstances, if they tried to get sea-room, instead of sitting there to be hopelessly battered by those mountains of ice. For only those who were exposed to the horror would believe how monstrously great these were.

By noon the next day, the four ships were out to sea and completely clear of the ice. But as soon as they were in a position to enjoy their own liberty, they began instead to worry about the safety of the rest of the fleet. Kneeling devoutly around their mainmasts, they humbly thanked God for having saved them and besought him to deliver their friends as well. And even in the midst of their extremities, while that gallant fleet and those valiant men were overwhelmed by the long and fearful continuation of their agonies, it pleased God to lower his merciful eyes and look down from heaven.

The next day, God sent them a more favourable wind from the west-northwest, which not only dispersed the ice, but offered the ships more scope and sea-room, so that by the following night they were happily united with the other four ships. The men now spent their time repairing the ships that had been most seriously bruised by the ice, setting up their topmasts, mending their sails and tackle, and stopping the leaks. Some merely complained of false stems being carried away and did nothing more than recount their recent experiences. I can truly declare that no men were ever more dangerously distressed or more mercifully delivered by God's providence. And both the battered ships and the exhausted men bore the marks of their ordeal. The whole fleet therefore moved off to seaward, resolved to stay there until the ice in Frobisher's Straits should either be melted by the sun or dispersed by the wind. When they were a fair distance off shore, they took in their sails and lay adrift.

On July 7, being still undaunted, we moved cautiously westward and sighted land which looked very much like the North Foreland. Many thought that it was, although others did not share this opinion.

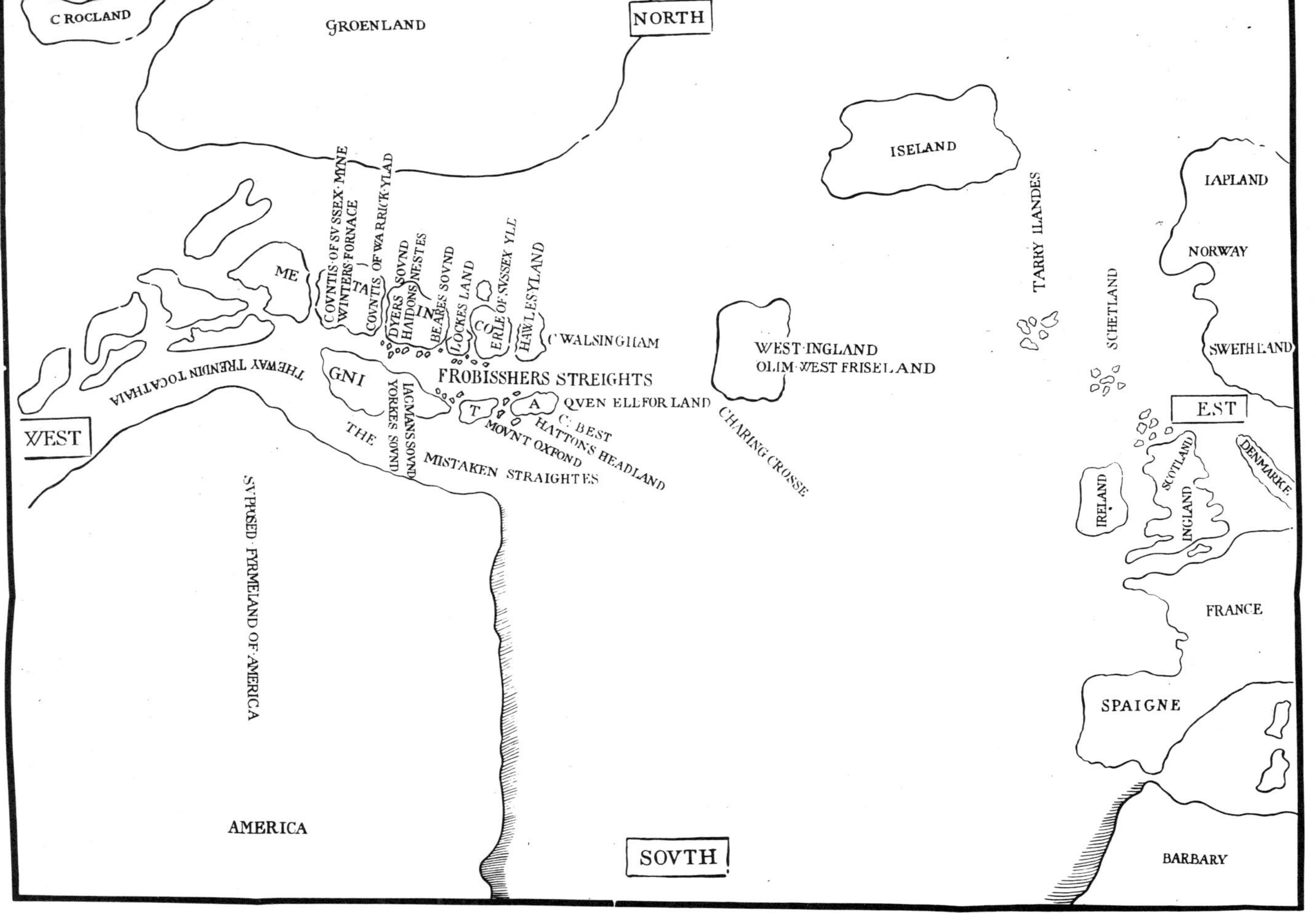

Beare's map of Frobisher's Straits

Courtesy of the Hakluyt Society

The matter, however, was not easily decided, because of a thick fog that hung along the coast for a long time and the snow which alters the shape of the land each year and hides the landmarks of the sailors. As the fog lasted for twenty days, our doubts increased and our position grew increasingly perilous. Although we thought that we were northeast of Frobisher's Straits, we were now carried southwestward of the Queen's Foreland by a swift and deceptive current sweeping down from the northeast. It carried us many miles off course, much farther than we would have thought possible. Since then, we have found the cause of our difficulties, which we will explain later.

Finally we reached a point of land which many of the men mistook for a place in Frobisher's Straits that had been named Mount Warwick. How the fleet had been shot so suddenly, and so far, up into the strait, even the most experienced sailors could not say. They thought it impossible that they could be so far out in their navigation, or that they could have completely overlooked such a powerful current on their earlier voyages. Many confessed, however, that they found the flood to be much swifter than they had formerly observed. It was truly wonderful to hear the roar of the tides in that place, and to see the water swirling around with such violence that our ships would sometimes be pivoted around when they were lying a-hull, as though they were in a whirlpool. And the noise of it all could be heard as far off as the noise of the waterfall at London Bridge.

While the fleet lay anxiously amidst that vast plain of floating ice, they knew not where they were; without the sun they had no way of calculating their latitude, nor could they see the coast with sufficient clarity to know if it looked familiar. The general, however, began seriously to question their position and sent his pinnace to each ship to get the opinions of the captains and masters. He was particularly interested in the opinion of James Beare, master of the *Anne Frances*, who had carefully drawn charts of the coast when he had been in the strait the year before. But the assembled opinions merely made the situation more doubtful, for Christopher Hall, chief pilot of the expedition, declared plainly and publicly, in the hearing of the whole fleet, that he had never seen that coast before. Unlike some of the men, he did not think that it could be any place in Frobisher's Straits, even though the similarity was so great that even the finest mariner might be deceived.

On July 10 some of the vessels lost sight of the admiral in the fog and thus lost contact with the rest of the fleet. Wandering back and forth, they tried to decide whether it were best to beat back to the open sea through great masses of ice, or to continue along an uncertain course in unknown waters that might be either a sea, bay, or strait. And in the fog and mists, they could not avoid the danger of rocks and broken grounds, which are so common in those parts of the world.

The vice-admiral, Captain Yorke, was one of those who lost contact with the admiral. Acting upon the opinion of the chief pilot, Christopher Hall, who was with him aboard the *Thomas Allen*, he headed back to the open sea, followed by two other vessels that were with him.

The captain of the *Anne Frances* also lost contact with the admiral and, being all alone, decided to move out to sea until clear weather would permit him to measure the altitude of the sun, and thus work out his latitude. With incredible hardship and peril he escaped to the open sea; but because of the continual threat of fog and ice, his men were frequently tempted to avoid the immediate danger by leaping onto an island of ice, and thus to die a more lingering death. Some of them hoped to save themselves by floating ashore on wooden chests. Others had decided to make rafts of the ship's hatches and to tie themselves and their gear to the rafts, and thus be towed ashore by the ship's boat, which itself would have held only half of the crew. Had they been fortunate enough to reach shore that way, they would either have died of starvation or been eaten themselves by the ravenous, bloody, and man-eating natives.

The rest of the fleet followed the general, who led them more than sixty leagues into the Mistaken Straits,[1] with a fair continent to starboard and a broad open sea ahead. The general was probably the first to discover the error and to realize that that was not the strait they had formerly explored. Yet he persuaded the fleet that they were in the old strait and on the right course. He did this, I suspect, because of his honourable desire to carry out further exploration; he simply wanted to induce the fleet to follow him. Some of the men reported later—and the general has since confessed—that had he not been responsible for the rest of the fleet, he both would and could have sailed on to the South Seas and settled once and for all the old question of a northwest passage to the riches of Cathay.

We believe that there is good hope of finding such a passage through the Mistaken Straits for the following reasons.

---

[1]Having mistaken Queen Elizabeth's Foreland (Resolution Island) for North Foreland (Hall's Island), Frobisher was actually in Hudson Strait. He named it Mistaken Straits when he realized his error.

1. The farther we sailed into the bay, sea, or strait, the wider we found it, and it is very likely that this condition continues endlessly. For after sailing up the strait some fifty or sixty leagues, we were not at all hindered by the ice that we found so troublesome in other places.

2. Also, the strait seems to have a marvellous great indraught or current, which sucks in most of the drifting ice and other things that float in the sea either to the north or the east, as we found through experience.

3. Here also we met with boards, laths, and several other things drifting on the sea. This was the wreckage of the *Dennis*, the bark that perished in the ice off the Queen's Foreland at the mouth of Frobisher's Straits. Because this debris originated so far away, it could not have been carried deeply into the Mistaken Straits by either wind or tide, but only by the force of that great current. For if it had been carried into the strait by the tide at flood, it would have been carried out again at ebb. And it could not have been carried in by the wind, because the wind usually blew in the contrary direction when it was blowing at all.

After careful observation, some of the men are convinced that in this strait the tide runs nine hours flood to three hours ebb, a difference which may be caused by that same current. For in most parts of the world, the tide ebbs and flows once every twelve hours, more or less, with six hours ebb and six hours flood. It would do the same thing here if it were not for the hastening current, which forces the flood to make its appearance an hour and a half early and to continue beyond its normal time by another hour and a half. Then the force of the ebb is so great that it can no longer be resisted; for according to the old saying, *Naturam expellas furca licet tamen usque recurrit.* (Although nature and natural causes be forced and resisted ever so much, yet at last they will have their own way again.)

4. Moreover, it is impossible that such great floods and currents, such high-swelling tides and uniformly deep waters, can be digested here without being unburdened into some open sea beyond this place. Therefore the possibility of a northwest passage somewhere in this area is increased.

We suspect that these great indraughts are caused by the reverberation and reflection of that same current that we crossed through after we left Ireland, and which I mentioned earlier. It comes from the Gulf of Mexico, washes the southwest coast of Ireland, then continues over the northeast parts of the world, such as Norway, Iceland, etc. Instead of finding a passage to an open sea that way, the current is augmented by another coming from the Scythian Sea and sweeping westward across Saint Nicholas Bay. Next, it is deflected back past the coasts of Greenland, and from there into Frobisher's Straits, which lie to the southwest of Greenland.

5. If that principle of philosophy be true which says that *Inferiora corpora reguntur a superioribus*, that is, that inferior bodies are governed, ruled, and carried after the manner and course of their superiors, then the water, being an inferior element, must needs be governed by the superior heavens, and so must follow the course of the heavenly bodies from east to west.

6. Every man who has written anything regarding this passage has doubted that it would be possible to return by the same route, because of a great downfall of water which they imagine to be someplace in the area. We found such a downfall in that place, yet nothing that would prevent our return, although it made that return difficult. For we were easily carried into the strait in one hour farther than we could sail out again in three. On another occasion, too, we found this current very deceptive; we were lying a-hull fifteen leagues off shore, so we thought, when suddenly we found ourselves within two leagues of the coast, contrary to all expectation.

The men who sailed farthest into the Mistaken Straits (with the mainland upon their starboard side) say that they met with a current that flowed out of Frobisher's Straits. Some members of our company also affirm that they sighted a continent on their port side when they had sailed sixty leagues into the strait. However, we could not see anything clearly, except some islands at the entrance. This whole stretch of coast seemed to be more fruitful and populous than any area we had yet explored, with better pasture and more deer, and more wild fowl, such as partridges, larks, sea-mews, gulls, wilmots, falcons, and tassel gentils, as well as ravens, bears, hares, foxes, and other things. One of the gentlemen of the company, Luke Ward, traded some merchandise there, exchanging knives, bells, looking-glasses, etc. with the people of the country for fowl, fish, bearskins, and such other things as the country provided. There also they saw some of the larger boats of the country with twenty people in each.

After the general had spent many days there and had experienced many dangers, he turned back. And while he was sailing along that coast, which was the back side of the supposed continent of America and the Queen's Foreland, he saw a great sound which appeared to go through into Frobisher's Straits. He therefore sent the *Gabriel*, on July 21, to see if it could get through the sound and meet him in the straits. This it did, proving, as we had suspected, that the Queen's Foreland was actually an island, as I think most of those continents will prove to be. And so the general departed towards the straits, thinking it high time now that he reach his destination and load the ships with ore. He still had to be very cautious, however, for while returning with the rest of the fleet, he got caught in the fog and entangled in the islands and broken grounds that lie off that coast. It was so bad that many of the ships passed over rocks that allowed them only half a foot clearance, as was seen at low tide. And because there was not enough wind for them to stem the flood and thus get clear of the rocks, they were forced to anchor with a double cable in over 100 fathom of water to avoid being swept back onto the rocks, where they would surely have perished. If God had not led us through these dangers as a merciful guide—and beyond the expectation of man—we would have been lost. Many times we were driven towards shore without any sight of land till we were almost shipwrecked upon it. This would happen, too, even while we had the boats out taking soundings ahead of the ships lest we strike something before we could see it. But then it pleased God to send us a brief patch of sunlight so that we could see and avoid the danger that had been hidden in darkness before, and would be presently again. Many times, also, when we were being driven ashore by fogs and currents, God would send us one prosperous breath of wind, just enough to double some headland and avoid the peril. And when we were beyond all hope, when every man was recommending himself to death and crying out: "Lord, help us now. Look down from heaven and save us sinners now, or else our deliverance will come too late," even then, the mighty Maker of heaven and our merciful God did deliver us. And those who have partaken of these dangers confess in their souls that God saved them even through miracles—may his name be praised evermore.

For a long time, the *Anne Frances* had been beating off and on before the Queen's Foreland, as she was unable to reach port because of the ice. She had tried many times, and at great danger, but the ice choked up the passage so thickly that it was impossible to enter. She had not seen any other ship since she had been separated from the rest of the fleet twenty days before, during a fog in the Mistaken Straits. Then, on July 23, she met seven of the fleet opposite a place in the strait called Hatton's Headland. The crew of the *Anne Frances* was comforted both by the end of their own isolation and by the knowledge that their friends were safe. At their meeting they hailed the admiral after the manner of the sea, joyously welcomed one another with thundering volleys of shot, and then settled down to a discussion of the things they had accomplished and the dangers they had escaped from.

On July 24 we met the *Frances of Foy*, which reported that she had fought her way out of the ice of the Mistaken Straits with great difficulty, and then had tried with equal difficulty to reach our destination in the Countess of Warwick's Sound. They also brought us the first news we had had of the *Thomas Allen* and the *Buss of Bridgewater*,[2] both of which had accompanied the *Frances of Foy*. They reported that they had left the *Thomas Allen* reasonably clear of the ice, but that there was some doubt about the other ship. When last seen, the *Buss* was in difficulties, and they themselves were so hard pressed that they could not go to her assistance. In addition, they told us that the *Gabriel* had got through the sound leading from the Mistaken Straits and the westernmost point of the Queen's Foreland into Frobisher's Straits, and had met them near the Cape of Good Hope.

On July 27 the *Buss* got out of the ice and joined the rest of the fleet, which was standing off and on under Hatton's Headland. She reported on all the accidents that had happened to them and all the dangers they had been exposed to, declaring their ship to be so leaky that they must of necessity seek out a harbour. For their stem had been pushed so far back into the hull that they were having trouble keeping themselves afloat, and had to pump 500 strokes in less than two hours, or half a watch. The crew was so exhausted with this work and with their recent dangers that they asked for help from the men of the other ships. Moreover, they declared there was nothing but ice and danger where they had come from, and that the strait was frozen solid, making it impossible for us to reach our destination in the Countess of Warwick's Sound.

When this report had spread throughout the fleet and was added to the memory of the dangers they had already escaped from, as well as to the prospect of those they were presently facing, the hearts of many brave men were filled with fear and terror. Some, as a result, began to grumble that the general was too wilful. Others wanted to find some nearby harbour so that the men might refresh themselves for a while and repair the damaged ships, while the north and northwest winds cleared a path for them by dispersing the ice. And still others, forget-

---

[2]That is, the *Ema. of Bridgewater*. The word "Buss" refers here to a type of vessel. There were two ships in Frobisher's fleet named *Emanuel* – the *Emanuel of Exeter* and the *Emanuel of Bridgewater*. Hence the confusion.

ting themselves and their duty, said that they might just as well be hanged when they got home as attempt the passage without hope of success and then perish in the ice.

The general, however, refused to open his ears to the peevish passions of any private persons, but concerned himself mainly with the public profit and his country's cause, disregarding even his own comfort and welfare. Knowing how little time there was left to load such a large number of ships with ore, he decided that he would either reach his destination or die in the attempt. And if it should indeed happen that he must perish amid the ice, then, when everything else had failed and all hope of recovery was gone, he would have all the ordnance well charged and would blow up himself, his crew, and all of Her Majesty's ships. And with this final peal of ordnance he would receive an honourable knell—instead of a proper burial—thinking it more fitting to end his life in this way than to have himself, his crew, or any of Her Majesty's ships fall into the hands of the base, bloody, and man-eating people who inhabit that region.

To appease the feeble passions of the more timid men, and to give himself more time in which the ice might be dissolved, he told the fleet that he was going to put into harbour. Then, while the ships lay off and on under Hatton's Headland, he sailed in among the islands with his pinnace, as though he was going to search for a harbour. In fact, he was searching for ore. Meanwhile, with the fleet lying off a lee shore without any clear idea of what they should be doing, a sudden and violent storm struck them from the south-southeast, piling the ice around them. Each ship was then forced to look after itself, to do what it thought best for its own safety. Most of the ships were so far up in the strait, so far to leeward, that they could not get out. Following the lead of the general, they took in their sails and lay a-hull amongst the ice. There the storm passed over them, causing them no great difficulty except for a short period.

The ships which did beat their way out to sea, however, were caught in a much more violent storm, and one which lasted much longer. For the nature of the place is such that it is subject to a variety of winds, which vary according to the situation of the great alps and mountains, with every mountain creating its own wind after the manner of a levant. During this storm the air became bitterly cold, and on July 26 so much snow fell that we could scarcely see one another, or even open our eyes to handle the ropes and sails. It piled up on the hatches of the ship till it was more than six inches deep, and it soaked the clothes of the sailors so thoroughly that a man who had five or six changes of clothing ended with scarcely one dry stitch. The cold and dampness, together with the constant labour of the poor men amidst the ice, caused considerable sickness throughout the fleet. This discouraged those men who had no previous experience in similar situations and persuaded all of us that where the summers were so unseasonable, the winter must indeed be extreme.

In spite of this cold air, the sun very often generated so much heat among the mountains that when there was no wind to bring us the cold air from the floating ice, we soon grew tired of the heat. Then, suddenly, a gust of wind came down from the hollows in the hills with such a blast of heat as we would feel if we entered a hot-house. And, just as suddenly, the wind would shift, and again blow cold.

During the storm, the *Anne Frances*, the *Moon*, and the *Thomas of Ipswich* were able to double about the cape of the Queen's Foreland, and so they headed out to sea. They thought it was safer to seek sea-room than to expose themselves to the hazards of the storm, the ice, and a lee shore. At the time, they were uncertain as to the general's personal intentions, and it was so dark that they could not see which way he went, or even see one another; so they headed for the safety of the open sea.

In spite of that great storm, the general followed his former resolution. He tried everything possible to reach his destination by a shorter route. Whenever he saw the smallest opening, he nipped in one side and out the other, and thus induced the fleet to follow where he so valiantly led. With incredible suffering and danger, he pushed his way through the ice till he finally reached the Countess of Warwick's Sound and dropped his anchor on July 31. At the entrance to the sound, when he thought he was out of danger, he struck a huge island of ice. As he had the anchor hanging from the cathead at the time, the force of the blow drove one of the flukes through the bows of the *Aid* below the waterline. This caused the ship to leak so badly that they prevented her sinking only with great difficulty.

When the general arrived at the sound, he found the *Michael*, with the lieutenant general, Captain Fenton, and the *Gabriel* riding at anchor there. The two ships had been missing so long that no one ever expected to see them again. So everyone rejoiced at the meeting, and they welcomed each other by firing the great guns, as is the custom at sea. After each group had discussed their recent experiences, they humbly knelt in prayer. And Mr. Wolfall, a learned man who had been appointed by Her Majesty's Council to be the expedition's minister, preached them a godly sermon. He particularly exhorted them to be thankful for their strange and miraculous deliverance. He reminded them, too, of the uncertainties of human life and urged them to be prepared, as resolute men should be, to accept with gratitude whatever situation a divine providence might place them in. This Mr. Wolfall was a man of substance at home, enjoying a fine living, an honest wife, well-behaved children, and a good reputation. He had agreed to go on that painful voyage because of his desire to convert the natives to Christianity, if at all possible, and thus to save their souls. He also hoped that an expedition which had started so auspiciously might be brought to a happy and prosperous conclusion, and was prepared to stay the whole year in Meta Incognita if that were necessary. Thus he may rightly be called a true pastor and minister of God's Word, for he did not hesitate to risk his own life for the welfare of his flock.

But let us return to Captain Fenton's company so that I can tell you of the dangers they were exposed to—although they were greater than can ever be expressed in writing. They reported that they had been gripped in the ice for almost twenty days, from the beginning of the storm about July 1 till about a week before the arrival of the general on July 26. And every hour of every day they were in danger and in fear of death. Their ship was pierced many times on both sides and had its false stem carried away by the battering of the ice. This ice pressed so closely around them that the men could walk for miles across its surface, and could even have reached shore if they wished. And if God had not provided for them and their needs, and if time had not made them cunning and wise enough to seek strange remedies for strange situations, they would never have escaped.

Among other devices, they would protect themselves from the threat of drifting ice by fastening themselves to one of the larger islands of ice and using it as a bulwark. In this way they anchored themselves to islands that were more than half a mile around and almost half a mile high. Finally, however, they would be forced to leave the pro-tection of their bulwark, because they would be surrounded by drifting ice, and this would bruise them severely if there was any swell to the sea. Then they would fasten the nose of their ship to the broadest and firmest slab of ice they could find and set all the sails. Having great power, the wind would drive the ship forward, and the great slab of ice would push the smaller pieces of ice aside. Having put its enemies to flight, the ship had a clear space for a while among those mountains of ice. One of those alps was measured and found to be sixty-five fathom high, and because of a general similarity was called Solomon's Porch. Some people think that those islands of ice have eight times as much hidden under water as is visible above, because of their monstrous weight. And strange things were seen amongst the ice, such as men walking, running, leaping, and shooting upon the high seas forty miles from land, without any ship or other vessel under them. In addition, there were rivers of fresh water running amidst the salt sea 100 miles from land! I know this is hard to believe, but many of the men leaped out of the ships and onto the islands of ice, where they ran up and down shooting at barrels with their calivers and at the large seals that used to sleep on the ice. And the reflection of the sun would melt the tops of the mountains of ice so that there would be small streams of water running down their sides. When some of these were joined together, they formed a brook that could have driven a mill.

Captain Fenton had reached the anchorage ten days before any of the others and had spent the time searching for ore; he found a large quantity, which proved to be of such quality that the mine was called Fenton's Fortune. He also explored about ten miles into the interior, but found neither town, nor village, nor any other indication that the country was inhabited. He reported that the land was just as barren as the other parts of the country they had seen. By this time, however, their supplies were so low that they decided to return to England if the fleet did not arrive within a week.

Following his arrival in the Countess of Warwick's Sound, the general immediately called a meeting of his council to discuss the things that had to be done. First, they had to locate a good body of ore so that the miners could be set to work. Then, regulations had to be drawn up for governing the entire company on shore. And finally, plans had to be made for erecting the fort which would house the men who were to live there for the following year. To deal with these and similar matters, it had been ordained by Her Majesty and the council that the general should appoint some of the senior captains and some of the gentlemen to advise him. The following were appointed:

> Captain Fenton
> Captain Yorke
> Captain Best
> Captain Carew
> Captain Philpot

To assist the captains in nautical matters, Christopher Hall and Charles Jackman were selected, both being very good pilots and skilled mariners. Hall was also chief pilot for the voyage, and Jackman was in charge of exploration. From our anchorage westward, Mr.

Selman was appointed notary, and was charged to keep a record of everything that happened there, so that an accurate report could be prepared if it pleased Her Majesty to require it.

On August 1 every captain was told that all such gentlemen, soldiers, and miners as were under his command were to be put ashore on the Countess of Warwick's Island. He was also to unload all of the food, tents, and other equipment necessary for mining the ore and loading the ships. When the men had been mustered and the food and equipment inspected, every man was set to work according to his place and office. The miners were told where to start work while the sailors unloaded the ships.

On August 2, to the sound of a trumpet, the general and his council proclaimed the orders that were to be observed by the company during their stay on the Countess of Warwick's Island. The following is a copy:

Orders set down by M. Frobisher Esquire, Captain General for the voyage to Cathay, to be observed of the company, during the time of their abode in Meta Incognita. Published the second day of August. Anno. 1578.

1. First, the general, in Her Majesty's name, orders and commands that no person or persons, with either boat or pinnace, shall go ashore for any reason, except to the Countess of Warwick's Island and to Winter's Furnace, without permission of the general or his deputies. And having permission, if they should happen to meet any of the country people, they shall neither trade nor fight with them until they have notified the general or his lieutenant.

2. No person whatsoever shall assay any metal, matter, or ore in the area now called Meta Incognita unless he shall be appointed by the general, or in his absence by his lieutenant, to do so. Nor shall any person take up and keep for his personal use any part or parcel of ore, precious stone, or other type of commodity to be had or found in that land, but as soon as he detect the same shall deliver it to the general or the lieutenant general. If any one fails to do this, he shall forfeit for each such ounce three times the value of any wages he would have received after the day of committing such an offence. He is also to receive such punishment as Her Majesty shall decide upon.

3. No ship or ships shall load any type of ore without permission of the general or of a deputy whom he shall appoint to view the ore and the loading.

4. All the masters of every ship or ships within the fleet shall, by next Monday at four o'clock in the morning, repair to the Countess of Warwick's Island with all or most of their company. There they shall select such places for loading and unloading of ore and other things as shall be most suitable for that purpose.

5. No person or persons within this service by sea or by land shall be caught swearing, brawling, or cursing, upon pain of imprisonment.

6. No person or persons, either by sea or land, shall draw his or their weapons in a quarrelsome manner to the intent to offend or disturb the peace of any person or persons within this service. Anyone so taken will immediately lose his right hand.

7. No person or persons shall wash their hands or any other things in the spring upon the Countess' Island where the water is used and preserved for the preparation of food, upon pain of receiving such punishment as the general or his lieutenant shall consider suitable. And for the better preservation and health of everyone, no person or persons shall do his easement anywhere except under the cliffs, where the sea may wash the same away; anyone so offending for the first time shall be imprisoned in the bilges for fourteen hours, and for the second time shall pay twelve pence.

8. No person or persons of any nature or condition shall cast out of their ship or ships any ballast or rubbish into the road where these ships are now riding, or may conveniently ride, within the sound, that might impair the road or the sound. They are to carry such ballast or rubbish to some spot where it will not offend. For each and every such offence, the ships shall forfeit the freight of one ton.

By me Martin Frobisher.

In the meantime, while the mariners plied their work, the captains searched for new mines, the goldfiners assayed the ore, the sailors unloaded their ships, and the gentlemen laboured heartily so as to set a good example and to honestly encourage the men. As a result, very little of the short time we could remain on the island was wasted.

On August 2 the *Gabriel* arrived with the news that the vice-admiral was at anchor near Mount Oxford, after being seriously distressed by the ice. By now the whole fleet, apart from the ship lost earlier, had arrived safely, except for the *Thomas Allen*, the *Anne Frances*, the *Thomas of Ipswich*, and the *Moon*. The absence of those four ships considerably hindered the work on the island, because they were carrying some of the best miners as well as some of the material that was needed to build the house.

On August 9 the general assembled the members of his council and started making plans for the erection of the house or fort for those who were going to winter there, so that the masons and carpenters might start work. But first he examined the bills of lading that showed what each ship was carrying and found that they had only the east and the south sides of the house. And even these were incomplete, for many pieces that were used as fenders had been broken while the ships were trapped in the ice. After due examination, it was also found that there was not enough of either beer or fuel for the 100 men who were supposed to winter there, because so much of it was in the ships which had not yet arrived. When Captain Fenton saw how scarce supplies really were, he offered to spend the winter there himself with only sixty men. They then asked the carpenters and masons how long it would take them to erect a smaller structure, one that would house the sixty men. If there were sufficient lumber, they said, it would require eight or nine weeks; however, they could remain in the area no more than twenty-six more days. It was agreed, therefore, that no one would be left there to spend the winter. Mr. Selman, the notary, was then asked to record their unanimous decision, so that Her Majesty, the Lords of the Council, and the Adventurers might be satisfied.

Since she had become separated from the fleet in the last storm, the *Anne Frances* had not been able to fight her way out through the last five leagues and thus get clear of the Mistaken Straits. For sometimes the wind was contrary, and almost always the ice surrounded her completely. And from that time—about July 27—she neither saw nor heard anything of the fleet until August 3, when she spotted a sail near Mount Oxford. When they could hail her, they learned that she was the *Thomas of Ipswich*, but had no news whatever of the rest of the fleet. Since she became separated from the others, she had been at sea, lying off and on in very foul weather and contrary winds, and had not seen any of the other ships. Then, shortly after they met, they again became separated, although the *Moon* managed to stay with the *Anne Frances*. These two continued to fight their way up the strait, hoping finally to reach their anchorage. With each attempt, they went as far as they could against contrary winds, foul weather, and ice. For when the weather was clear and without fog, then the wind was usually contrary; and with a favourable wind from the east or the south, there was such a thick fog and dark mist that either they could not find a path through the ice, or else the ice was so thick that it was impassable. And when it was calm, on the other hand, the tide would bring the ice so suddenly upon them that they were in serious danger without any means of escape.

By August 6 the two vessels had fought their way up as high as Leicester Point. They expected to find the south shore clear of ice, and so to be able to move up the strait towards their destination. But they were becalmed and forced to lie a-hull out in the great bay at the mouth of the Mistaken Straits, where they were dangerously beset by the ice that was piled about them by the swift tide. In trying to avoid the ice in the thick weather, the *Anne Frances* lost sight of the other two ships. They were seriously distressed also, as they reported later, and tried to signal their plight by shooting off their ordnance, which the others could not hear. Even if they had been able to hear, they could have rendered no assistance, as they were fully occupied in getting out of their own difficulties.

During that period, the *Moon* was heaved out of the water by the ice and sprung a great leak as a result. The *Thomas of Ipswich* and the *Anne Frances* were both sorely bruised also, having their false stems torn away and their hulls pierced. They were now faced with continual dangers, contrary winds, and the knowledge that they could not remain much longer in that region. Besides that, the rigging froze so hard that a man could not handle it without cutting his hands. They were also concerned over the safety of the fleet, for they thought it would have been impossible for it to reach its destination. They believed this because of what they had seen themselves and what they had heard from the ships that had attempted the passage, which reported that the strait was frozen solid. As a result, it was decided that they must now look to their own safety. The officers of the other two ships therefore asked the captain of the *Anne Frances* to discuss the matter with them. When he agreed, Captain Tanfield of the *Thomas of Ipswich*, with his pilot, Richard Coxe, and Captain Upcot of the *Moon*, with his master, John Lakes, came aboard the *Anne Frances* on August 8 for consultation. As soon as they were assembled in the captain's cabin, certain doubts were raised. The more timid mariners, exhausted by the continual labours that were brought on by their former extremities, wished to return homeward. For God had already given them so many warnings, and delivered them from so many perilous situations, that they no longer wished to tempt him. They preferred losing both wages and freight to continuing along such

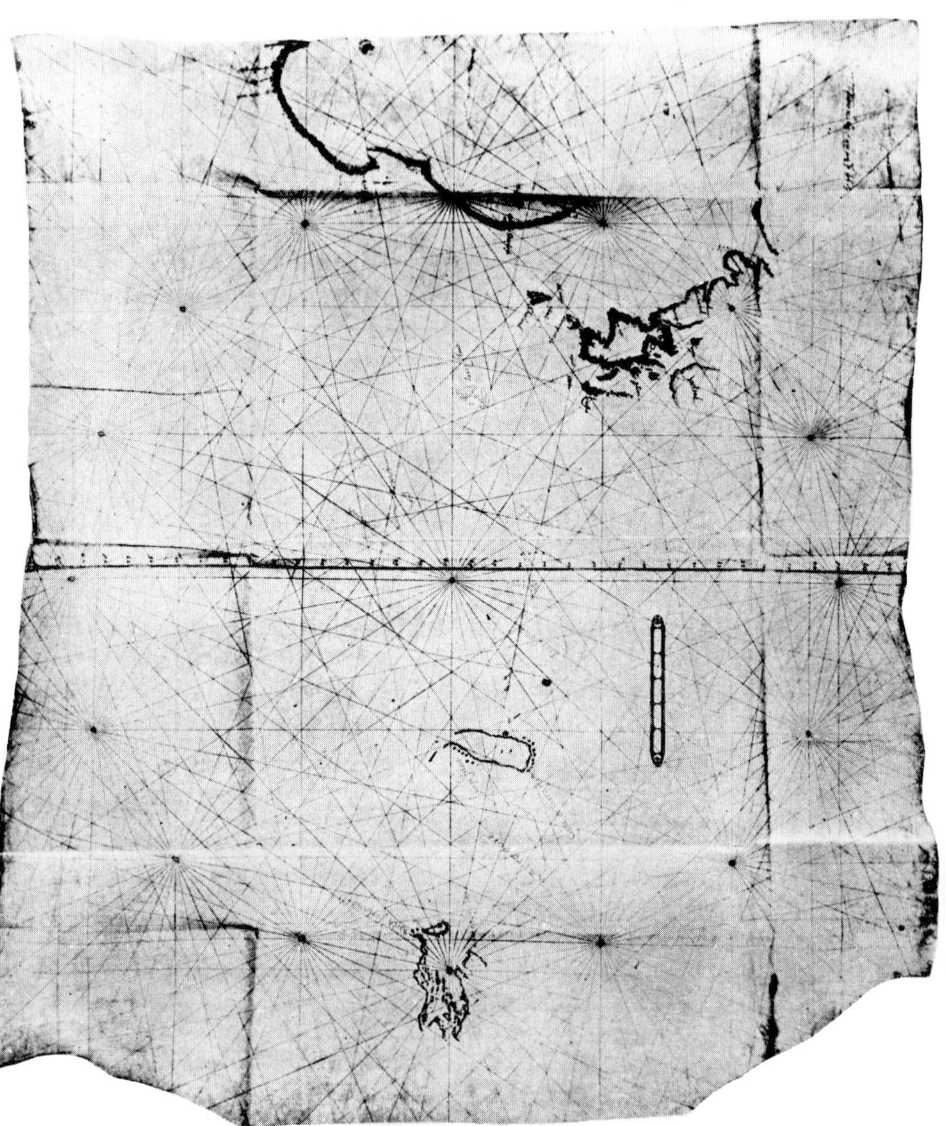

Borough's map. This was the original chart on which Frobisher marked his discoveries. From the Stefansson edition of *The Three Voyages of Martin Frobisher.*

Courtesy of Da Capo Press, Inc.

a desperate path. And their ships were so leaky and the crew so weary that they must of necessity go into some harbour, so as to mend the one and refresh the other.

It was argued, on the other hand, that to enter any harbour in the area would actually be much more dangerous. For if they were lucky enough to escape the rocks when they entered, they would still be exposed to the pressure of the ice when they were inside. Carried in and out of most of the harbours, this ice could very easily sever their anchor cables, drive them upon the shore, and thus get them into serious difficulties. In addition, the coast is so broken up and rocky, especially in the entrance to every harbour, that the hazards can never be charted, no matter how often the channel is sounded. For the bottom of the sea is very similar to the land and is made up of hills, dales, and jagged rocks, which make it impossible to know the depth by soundings. Thus you can sound upon the side or lower part of a hill or rock under water and have forty fathom; and before you have time to heave the lead again, you are aground, to your utter confusion.

Another argument against entering a harbour was the dropping temperature, which threatened to freeze up the smaller sounds and bays. For every night a film of ice would form even upon the water that was within the ship. It seemed safer, therefore, to stand off and on at sea than to enter a bay where a sudden frost might trap them for an entire year.

After discussing these matters from every possible angle, the captain of the *Anne Frances* told the company that any question of returning home then was so dishonourable that he would not even consider it. He said that he would not return till he knew for sure what had happened to the fleet. He had to know whether the men were living or dead, and whether any of them had reached the Countess of Warwick's Sound, as he was sure they would if they remained alive. Any other course of action, he said, would show that they were lacking in either courage or discretion. And thus he would not return home till he had done everything possible to find out what had happened to the general. He reminded the company that he had aboard his ship a knocked-down pinnace of some five tons burden. This was intended for the use of the men who were going to winter in the country. If they could find some means of assembling it, the captain offered to take the pinnace himself and explore ahead of the ships to see if there was any passage that they might follow. This way, they would also find out if any of the other ships were there.

On the other hand, he did recognize that most of his company were anxious to put into some harbour, and he was willing to consider their position for a number of reasons. First, he thought it might be a good idea to search the bays and sounds along the coast where some of the ships might have taken refuge. For any ships that were leaky or seriously bruised by the ice during the last storm might have preferred the doubtful protection of a poor harbour to the known hazards that awaited them amongst the ice. It was in that place, too, that the *Anne Frances* had last seen the fleet, and even then it was probably looking for shelter. It was likely, also, that they might find some snug harbour that could be useful at a later date. It might even be possible to find a mine in the area. This would be particularly helpful because it would enable them to load their ships in less time, and to reach the open sea more rapidly and by a better route. And it would not matter how thickly the strait was cluttered with ice. Thus they would hope to locate either the fleet, a mine, or a convenient harbour; and any one of those would offer some hope and comfort to men who were otherwise without comfort. Even if they were so unfortunate that they could accomplish nothing, they would still not leave that coast so long as it was possible to remain there, but would stand off and on at sea. Therefore, his final conclusion was this:

The *Thomas of Ipswich* and the *Moon* were to stay as close as possible to the *Anne Frances*, and as true Englishmen and faithful friends they were to protect and assist one another. The next morning, each ship was to send its boat with a good pilot to search for and sound a safe harbour for the ships. When they found a suitable harbour and a convenient spot for the purpose, they would assemble the pinnace. And then the captain of the *Anne Frances* would use it to explore up into the strait.

In spite of these arrangements, the *Thomas of Ipswich* got separated from the other ships the following night and sailed for home a short time afterwards. As it turned out, this was very much against the wishes of Mr. Tanfield, the captain. This was demonstrated later on when he was examined by the Lords of Her Majesty's Most Honourable Privy Council. For it was established there that the pilot, Mr. Coxe, had persuaded the crew to return home against the wishes of the captain. And the captain of the *Anne Frances* says that at their meeting, Captain Tanfield told him that he was suspicious of pilot Coxe, and that he was not convinced of his sense of duty, his manhood, or his determination.

Even though the *Thomas of Ipswich* was no longer with them, the captain of the *Anne Frances* still decided to go ahead with his plan.

Accompanied by the skiff from the *Moon*, he took his own boat to search among the islands that lie under Hatton's Headland to see if he could find a convenient harbour, an ore deposit, or any sign of the fleet. His ships, meanwhile, were standing off and on at sea. Most of the sounds that he examined were studded with rocks and broken grounds, yet there was one that was perhaps suitable, so they examined it a second time.

There the captain found a large black island that looked interesting, and so he signalled the other boat and they rowed over to inspect it. When they got there, they found a vast quantity of the same kind of ore that they had taken to England the previous year. There was so much of the ore on the island that if the quality was as good as the quantity, there was enough to satisfy all the gold gluttons in the world. Because of his good fortune, the captain named it after himself, calling it Best's Blessing. Then he returned to his ship with the good news on that August 9, about ten o'clock at night; he was heartily welcomed by his companions, who had not been in the best of spirits and were hoping for some good fortune at his hands.

As the weather was reasonably fair the next day, August 10, they moved the ships into the harbour, with the boats sounding out the channel ahead of them. In spite of the fact that they sounded the channel over and over again, the *Anne Frances* hit a submerged rock and lay there more than half dry until the next high tide. Then, by God's almighty providence, and contrary to almost all expectation, she floated free. Meanwhile, she had been propped up by the main yard to prevent her from upsetting and endangering the whole company. She was still so bruised from her encounter with the rocks that it took more than two thousand strokes to pump her dry. The *Moon*, meanwhile, entered the harbour in perfect safety, where she anchored beside the *Anne Frances* to offer whatever assistance was necessary.

While the sailors were rummaging their ships and mending any gear that was broken, the miners started gathering up ore, and the carpenters started to assemble the pinnace. But two essential things were missing: certain main timbers that are called "knees", and which give any boat its strength, and nails to fasten the planks together. Fortunately there was a smith on board, but he had none of the tools that were needed to make nails. As a result, he was forced to use a gun-chamber as an anvil, a pickaxe instead of a sledge-hammer, and two small bellows instead of a large blacksmith's bellows. Because they lacked small iron bars to fashion the nails from, they had to break up their grid-iron, tongs, and fire-shovel.

On August 11 the captain and master of the *Anne Frances* climbed to the top of Hatton's Headland, which is the highest point in all the straits. They wanted to take a look at the surrounding countryside, to draw a map of the area, to see how much ice was still left in the strait, and, finally, to see what minerals or fruit the soil might yield. Because of the respect which the captain owed to the honourable name of Hatton, a name which he himself had bestowed on that spot the previous year, he now erected a column or cross upon the highest point of the headland in token of Christian possession. There is a lot of black ore at that place, and a variety of interesting stones.

On August 17 the officers and men hunted and killed a great white bear, which turned upon them and fiercely assaulted twenty armed men. For many days afterwards, he kept them in fresh meat.

After many difficulties, the pinnace was finally assembled by August 18, and Captain Best was determined to carry out the plan that he had decided upon earlier. Some of the men, however, argued strongly against such a course, especially the carpenter who had assembled the pinnace. He said that he would not risk his life in that vessel for 500 pounds, because it lacked some of its principal knees and timbers and hung together only by the strength of the nails.

Those words tended to discourage some of the men who were to go along. Therefore the captain, who was not totally addicted to his own opinion, saw how it might appear later if some misfortune were to happen. So he called a meeting of the master mariners whose opinions he valued most, and told them how important it was for him to locate the general. He wanted to see Captain Frobisher for several reasons, but particularly to have the quality of the ore tested, for he had no assurance that it was, in fact, ore. It merely looked like ore. To carry it to England without having it assayed might mean that they were carrying nothing but stones. The captain, therefore, asked the men for their plain and honest opinion as to whether or not the pinnace was suitable for the project. They replied that if proper care was taken of the ice and foul weather, the pinnace might just suffice. At this point, the mate of the *Anne Frances*, John Gray, volunteered his services, and this prompted several of the men to follow his example.

On August 19 Captain Best, Captain Upcot of the *Moon*, and eighteen men set out on the voyage, leaving their ships at anchor with everything ready to take on a load of ore. In spite of the fact that there was little wind, they moved west along the southern shore, sometimes with oars, for more than thirty leagues. They intended to follow the shore to the farthest and narrowest part of the strait, where they would cross to the north shore, and then to follow that coast back to the Countess of Warwick's Sound. If the fleet was not there, they would search the entire coast for any vessels that might have been damaged by the ice or rocks and thus might be in need of assistance. For they felt it was highly probable that some of the fleet had been cast away and compelled to forage amongst the cold cliffs.

When they were about forty leagues up the strait, they put over towards the north shore, which was a dangerous crossing because their boats were so small. And then a sudden squall forced them to search for a safe anchorage at night among the rocks and broken grounds of Gabriel's Island, which is west of the Countess of Warwick's Sound. When they landed there, they found some large stones that had been set up by the natives, and so the crew fashioned many crosses of stone to show that Christians had been there. On August 22 they sighted the Countess' Sound, having a clear view of it from the top of a hill. As they followed the north shore, they noticed some smoke coming from the base of a hill, and as they got closer they could see some people waving what appeared to be either a flag or a pennant. Because the natives used to wave things when they saw our boats, the men suspected that these might be natives too. When the men got closer, they could see some tents, and could see also that the pennant was of mingled colours, black, and white after the English fashion. No ship could be seen, however, nor was there much probability of there being a harbour within five or six leagues of the place. As there was no reason for any of our party to be there, the men did not know what to make of it. They feared that some of the ships had been driven up the strait by the storm and mists and had been wrecked in that maze of ice and shattered islands, and that their crews had either been killed or captured by the natives, who then used the flag or pennant to lure others to their destruction. So Captain Best and his men decided to recover the pennant—if, indeed, it was a pennant—from those base, cruel, and man-eating people, or to die in the attempt. One of the men promised himself that he would make a pair of garters of that pennant, another a scarf, and a third said that he would make a cord to hang his whistle on. In the end, however, they saw that the people on the shore were Englishmen, and thought they had lost their ships and were gathered together for protection. The company on shore, meanwhile, thought that the captain had lost *his* ship and was using his tiny pinnace to try to locate the fleet. Thus each group was led to suspect the worst.

As he approached the shore, the captain ordered the men to make sure that the pinnace remained afloat. He was afraid that the men on shore might seize it out of desperation, for in such situations all men will try to save themselves first. The two parties hailed each other in the nautical manner, and they each replied that all was well. Then there was a sudden and joyful shout, a great flinging up of caps, and a mighty volley of musketry to welcome one another. And it was most strange indeed to see how pleased everyone was that they were safe after such strange and incredible dangers. Yet even though their dangers were great, their God was greater.

The men on shore were working on some new mines that Captain Yorke had found when he arrived there a short time before. He named them the Countess of Sussex Mine. After conferring with his friends there, the captain of the *Anne Frances* left for the Countess of Warwick's Sound to report to the general and to have the goldfiners assay the ore which he had aboard. The general told him to return to his ship, load it with the ore that he himself had found (and which, incidentally, had proved to be very rich), and then bring it to the Countess of Warwick's Sound.

On August 13 all of the captains attended a meeting with the general aboard the *Aid*, where a number of things were discussed—and duly recorded by the notary—regarding the next year's expedition. The next day, the fourteenth, the general set out with two pinnaces, accompanied by Captain Best with his pinnace, to see if he could capture any of the cannibals who had shown themselves several times. Frequently, a company of seven or eight boats would appear, acting as though it intended to attack the small group of our men working there in the mine. But after they saw some of our ships riding at anchor there, they never showed themselves again. They were amazed both by the ships themselves and by the number of men in our party. Our men, therefore, tried to intercept some of them by circling around the island where they lived, but the natives must have had a lookout on the top of the mountains, because they sneaked away before our men could get near them. In their haste they left behind them one of their large darts, which we found near their tents and caves. Although the general was very anxious to capture some of them to take back to England, the natives had grown more wary since their former losses and would never come within our grasp.

That night, about midnight, Captain Best headed across the strait towards Hatton's Headland, about fifteen leagues away. He reached the *Anne Frances* on August 25 to the great comfort of the men, as they had been expecting him for a long time and had already rigged and loaded the ships. He therefore left the next morning for the Countess of Warwick's Sound, where he arrived on the twenty-eighth. On the way, he put his miners ashore at Beare's Sound so that ore could be gathered together as rapidly as possible, for some of the ships were behind schedule with their loading, and time was quickly running out.

On August 30 the *Anne Frances* was brought aground to mend eight great leaks that had been caused by the rocks and ice. On that same day, the masons finished a house which Captain Fenton had had them build of lime and stone upon the Countess of Warwick's Island. The house was built so that next year we might see how it stood up over the winter—whether it would be overwhelmed by the snow, broken up by the frost, or dismembered by the natives. And to allure those brutish and uncivil people to courtesy (for we intended to return), we left a variety of English toys in the house. We left such things as knives and bells, which they are particularly delighted with, the knives because they are useful, and the bells because they are pleasant. We also left pictures of men and women in lead, men on horseback, looking-glasses, whistles, and pipes. In addition, we built an oven in the house and baked some bread, which we left there for them to see and taste.

We buried the timber for the fort that we intended to build, together with many barrels of meal, peas, grist, and several other valuable things that were part of the provisions of the men who had planned to spend the winter there. In their place, we loaded the ships with ore, which we thought was far more valuable. We also sowed peas, corn, and other grain, so that next year we would know how fruitful the soil was on the island.

Mr. Wolfall preached a godly sermon on Winter's Furnace and then celebrated a communion upon the land, attended by Captain Best and many other gentlemen, soldiers, sailors, and miners. This celebration of divine mystery was the first sign, seal, and confirmation of Christ's name, death, and passion ever known in that part of the world. Mr. Wolfall also preached and offered communion at other times and in other ships, because the entire company could never be assembled in one place.

As the fleet was now ready for loading, the general called a meeting of the gentlemen and captains and told them that he was anxious to attempt some further exploration. He told them that he meant to return home not only with his ships loaded with gold ore—with God's help—but also with proof that he had made some further discoveries. But they had already spent a lot of time following the Mistaken Straits far to the westward. It could not be said, therefore, that no discoveries had been made during the voyage, for they had already increased the hope of a passage that way. Still, if there was something else that could be done, the captains were quite prepared to carry out any orders the general should give them. After a lengthy discussion, however, it was agreed that the whole thing was impossible and that they should make plans for returning homeward, for the following reasons. First, the fogs and mists, the continually falling snow, and the stormy weather that they were commonly vexed with were increasing daily and suggested that winter was almost upon them. Second, it was freezing so hard every night that, if they should be trapped in the sound by contrary winds, it was very likely that they would be frozen in for the whole winter. And as they were completely unprepared for such an eventuality, it would mean their utter destruction. And, finally, there was very little left to drink throughout the fleet, because of leakage. They had lost both the beverage that was provided for the wintering party, and that of several ships. Many of the men found, to their grief, that there was nothing to drink on the homeward voyage but water. The leakage and waste were caused by the great weight of the timbers and coal, which lay so heavily upon the barrels that the hoops were broken, bruised, and rotted away.

The general therefore told the gentlemen and captains to look to their duties and said that by a given day they should be ready to sail for home. He himself, meanwhile, took the pinnace and went exploring farther up the strait to the northward. By Beare's Sound and Hall's Island he found that the land was not firm, as he had supposed, but was broken up into a series of islands like an archipelago. So with this and other information which he kept to himself, he returned to the fleet. On his arrival back at the Countess' Sound, he started making arrangements for the homeward voyage; but first he proclaimed certain articles for keeping the vessels in the proper order and on the right course during their return trip. These articles, which were delivered to every captain, were as follows:

Articles set down by Martin Frobisher, Esquire, Captain General of the whole fleet appointed for the Northwest discoveries of Cathay, published and made known to the fleet for the better observing of certain orders and courses during its return homeward.

1. First and principally, he charges and commands, by virtue of Her

Majesty's Commission and in Her Majesty's name, that every captain and captains, master and masters of the said fleet do diligently and carefully keep company with the admiral, and under no circumstances do separate themselves willingly during their return. Those who do shall forfeit their freight, shall receive such punishment as Her Majesty shall prescribe, and shall be responsible for any losses or damage that shall result from their action. And to make sure that the ships stay together, the general charges and commands that each of the masters of those ships shall speak with the admiral once every day if it may conveniently be done. The penalty for failing to comply with this order will be the forfeiting of one ton of freight to Her Majesty for every day of failure.

2. That every master in the said fleet shall observe all such articles as were drawn up and published by the general in Her Majesty's name, and delivered to every ship when they were outward bound.

3. That the captains and masters of every ship do proclaim and make known to their company that no person or persons within the said fleet shall take or keep to his own use or uses any ore or stones of any quantity whatsoever. As soon as they are found, all such ore or stones shall be turned over to the captain for delivery to those officers that the general shall appoint to receive them. The penalty for those who are found guilty of keeping ore or stones to their own use will be loss of his or their wages, and treble the value of such ore or stones. One half of such fines will be given to the man who apprehended the guilty person, the other half to Her Majesty. And in addition, any one found guilty of such an offence shall be apprehended as a felon.

4. That no person or persons shall convey or carry out of any ship or ships any ore, stone, or other commodity that was found in Meta Incognita before they arrive at the appointed place, which is against Dartford Creek in the Thames River. And having arrived there, none shall be delivered to any person or persons except such as shall be appointed by Her Highness' Most Honourable Privy Council. The penalty for any infraction shall be the same as is mentioned above.

5. During the outward voyage, I landed on Friesland with some of the men in an area that I named West England, and from which some of the men brought stones, ore, and other things. Because they might employ some devious means of conveying this material ashore, I therefore charge them as follows: Each person in the said fleet is to deliver, or cause to be delivered, all ore, stones, and other things found both

there in West England and here in Meta Incognita to the captain or captains of every ship or ships, who will deliver them in turn to the general. The penalty for any infraction shall be the same as is mentioned above.

6. If any ship or ships shall be separated from the admiral in bad weather, and shall then fall, or be in danger of falling, into the hands of an enemy, such ship or ships, before being captured, shall throw overboard all maps and charts of the newly discovered lands, and all other references to it.

7. If any ship or ships shall be separated from the fleet or the admiral in bad weather, and shall afterward arrive at any port in England, then it, or they, shall not leave that port, but shall notify Michael Lok, Treasurer of the company. He will consult with the Lords of the Privy Council, and they, in turn, will decide what should be done.

8. Sundry of the fleet's companies have been issued crowbars, sledgehammers, picks, shovels, spades, hatchets, axes, and other instruments that are used for mining; many of the same instruments were also left at the Countess of Sussex Mine by the crew of the *Aid*, and have not yet been returned by the miners who were working there. All of these tools belong to the right honourable and worshipful company. I therefore order all captains and masters to inform their companies that all such instruments must be delivered aboard the admiral under such penalty as is expressed in Article 3.

By me Martin Frobisher.

The Return Voyage

Having received articles and instructions for the homeward journey, and all other things being in good order, the fleet left the Countess of Warwick's Sound on the last day of August, except for the *Judith* and the *Anne Frances*. These stayed behind to take on fresh water and joined the fleet next day, where it was lying off and on at the entrance to Beare's Sound. It was waiting there for the general, who had gone ashore to see to the loading of the two barks and the *Buss of Bridgewater*, and to make sure that the men and their gear were brought aboard smartly. Most of the men from the *Anne Frances* were also ashore, and so the captain went to fetch them in his pinnace on September 1. As soon as they had landed, however, the wind became so strong that the ships at sea were in serious danger; some of them had hardly raised their anchors when they were threatened with utter destruction. Captain Carew and his men in the *Hopewell*, for example, could not tell which was the greater danger, the rocks which threatened them on one side or the jagged slabs of drifting ice on the other. And they feared they were surely wrecked when the ice passed so near them that it touched their bowsprit.

Because the sea was running so high, the men on shore were not able to reach their ships in the small pinnaces; nor were the ships able to wait for them, because of the outrageous winds and the swelling seas. The general, therefore, sent the captain and the men from the *Anne Frances* aboard the *Buss of Bridgewater* for the night, while he took the rest of the men aboard the barks. But their numbers were so great, and the provisions of the barks were so scanty, that they were exceedingly crowded. They fully expected that the weather would be fair the next morning, and thus enable them to return to their ships. But the following day was actually worse, for the storm had increased in violence, the sea had grown higher, and the fleet was nowhere in sight.

At this point, the men began to have serious doubts as to their safety; for the *Buss of Bridgewater*, which was best fitted to assist them, and in which they placed their greatest hopes, was riding so far to leeward of the harbour's mouth that they could not work it out to sea, because of the rocks that were between them and the wind. And the barks were already so crowded with men, and so slenderly furnished with provisions, that they had scarcely enough meat to last six days.

In the morning the general put to sea in the *Gabriel* to search for the fleet, leaving the *Buss of Bridgewater* and the *Michael* behind in Beare's Sound. The *Buss* tried to get to windward by turning in the narrow channel inside the harbour; but she was pushed farther to leeward and forced to anchor among a number of rocks, where there was the possibility that she would never be able to get out. The *Michael* had started to follow the general and was unable to assist the *Buss*, much as she wanted to. Meanwhile, the captain of the *Anne Frances* was left with a hard choice: he could either throw in his lot with the *Buss of Bridgewater*, which looked as if she might never be able to leave, or else he could have his tiny pinnace towed through those raging seas at the stern of the *Michael*. For the bark was not able to take even half of his men on board, and his situation was thus particularly perilous.

The captain, then, resolving to commit himself and his men to the mercies of God and that raging sea, was towed astern the *Michael*, until, after many miles, they saw the *Anne Frances* sailing hard under their lee. The sight was a great comfort to them all, for without the help of that ship, a great number of men would surely have starved to death in that overcrowded bark. Because the master of the *Anne Frances* was sincerely concerned with the welfare of his captain, as well as with his duty towards his general, he did not even think of leaving. On the contrary, he steadfastly rode out the night, in spite of the fact that his position was hazardous, a storm was raging, and all of the other ships were gone. As soon as the men had boarded the ship, the pinnace literally fell apart and sank at the stern of the *Anne Frances*, taking with it all of the men's gear. She had been weakened by the towing and sorely bruised by the pounding sea, but the men—as God willed—were all saved.

During that storm, many of the vessels were dangerously distressed, and most of them were widely scattered. About twenty boats and pinnaces were lost, as were several men who were washed overboard. Many of the masts and main yards were sprung; and with the continual frosts and dew, all of our ropes had grown so rotten that they were falling apart. Yet thanks be to God, all of the ships arrived safely at a number of different ports in England about October 1. The escape of the *Buss of Bridgewater* was a great marvel, as she had been left behind in Beare's Sound, where it looked as if she might never escape. She was forced to feel her way northward through an unexplored channel, full of rocks, that led to the back side of Beare's Sound. From there, fortunately, she found her way into the North Sea; this was a very dangerous passage, but necessity, which knows no law, forced them to master it. This North Sea is the body of water that lies behind the land on the north side of Frobisher's Straits. The region was first explored by the general in his pinnace. Later on, some of the men discovered a great foreland there at a place where there was also a good possibility of a fine passage to the South Sea.

On the homeward voyage, the *Buss of Bridgewater* discovered a large island southeast of Friesland and sailed along its coast for three days.[3] It seemed to be a fruitful, well-wooded land, and altogether a fine country.

---

[3]This "island" was sighted many times over the years, and was reported to be very rich in sea-mammals and codfish. In 1675 it was granted to the Hudson's Bay Company for a payment of £65. During the summer the Company sent the *Rupert* to search for it, but to no avail. It has still not been found.

During the entire voyage, no more than forty men were lost, not a particularly large number considering the size of the fleet and all the strange and wonderful things that happened.

End of the Third Voyage.

A General and Brief
Description of the Country,
and Condition of the People
which are found in Meta Incognita.

Having sufficiently and truly recorded the circumstances and details of everything that happened during the three voyages of our worthy general, Captain Frobisher, it should not be impertinent now if I make some comments on the nature of the country we call Meta Incognita and the condition of the inhabitants.

Concerning the topographical description of the area, it was found during the last voyage that Queen Elizabeth's Foreland, as well as the rest of the south shore of Frobisher's Straits, is not part of the American mainland, as we had formerly thought. It is a series of islands and broken grounds. In my opinion, the north side of the strait will turn out to be another series of islands and broken grounds when it is more fully explored. And the men who sailed more than sixty leagues into the Mistaken Straits—as mentioned during the third voyage—were positive they had seen the American mainland to the south. I think that this will prove to be true also.

These islands and broken lands are very numerous and seem to form an archipelago. The individual islands differ greatly in size and form, as well as in richness, colour, and soil; but they are all very high and mountainous, and most parts remain covered with snow during the entire summer. The north side of the strait is less mountainous and snow-covered than the south and is more richly clothed with grass. This may be caused by the fact that the south side receives all the snow that the cold winds and piercing airs bring out of the north, while the northern shore receives warm blasts of milder air from the south. This may also be the reason that the natives are more plentiful along the north shore than along the south, as was suggested by our experience.

I think these people are some kind of Tartars; they are the same kind of people, and have the same conditions of life, as those who live to the northeast of Moscow and are called Samoyeds. They were named Samoyeds by their neighbours, the Russians, for in the tongue of Moscow, that word means "eaters of themselves". I have a friend with long experience among these Samoyed and other people of the northeast, and in fact I once travelled with him to the Moscow area; and he tells me that the people of the northeast and the people of the northwest are very much alike. They are the colour of a ripe olive, but how they got that way when they were born in such a cold climate, I refer to the judgment of others, for at birth they are of the same colour and complexion as the Americans who dwell at the equator.

These men are very active and nimble. They are a strong people, and very warlike, as we saw in our fight upon the hilltops, when they would often show themselves in threatening posture, dashing about very nimbly, and managing their bows and arrows with great dexterity. They wear coats made of seal, deer, bear, fox, and rabbit skins, and some garments made of bird skins, finely sewn and compacted together. We took some of each kind of clothing that we found in their tents and brought them back to England with us. In summer they wear their clothing with the hair side outward, and on occasion go naked because of the heat. But in winter, as they indicated by signs, they wear four or five layers of clothing, with the hair turned inward for greater warmth. It appears from this that the temperature there is not indifferent, but is either fervently hot or extremely cold, and far more excessive in both qualities than would be suggested by the latitude. For it is colder in Meta Incognita than it is in Wardhouse on the route to Saint Nicholas in Muscovy, which is more than 70° north. The reason for this difference may be that Meta Incognita is frequented and vexed with eastern and northeastern winds, which are intolerably cold because of the sea and the ice. This may also explain why the strait was so jammed with ice this year. Thus it is very likely that the weather will be both more uniform and more temperate farther into the strait.

By nature, the native people are very subtle and quick-witted; they readily grasp the meaning of the signs we make, and in reply make signs that we can clearly understand. For example, if they have not seen the thing you ask them about, they will wink or cover their eyes with their hands, as though to say that it has been hidden from their sight. And if they do not understand the question you ask them, they will cover their ears. If we ask them, they will teach us the names of different things in their language, and they learn very quickly from us. Above all else, they delight in music. No matter what tune you sing, they will keep time with their voices, heads, hands, and feet, and then they will sing the same tune themselves. With great delight, they will row in our boats with our oars and keep a true stroke with the sailors.

They live in caves in the earth, and hunt for their dinners even as the bears and other wild beasts do. They eat raw flesh and fish and will not refuse any meat, no matter how rotten it may be. They are desperate in a fight, sullen in nature, and ravenous in their manner of feeding. Their sullen and desperate nature became manifest when a number of them were trapped by our men on the top of a high cliff where there was no hope of escaping. Fnding themselves distressed in this way, they chose to cast themselves over the cliff and into the sea, where they would be battered and drowned, rather than yield themselves to the mercies of our men.

To offend their enemies and kill their prey, these people use darts, slings, and bows and arrows; most of the arrows are headed with sharp stones or bones, but some are headed with iron. Among themselves, they are exceedingly friendly and kind-hearted, lamenting greatly the death or injury of their fellows. And when they part one from another, they express their grief with mournful songs and dirges. They are very modest about betraying the secrets of nature, and very chaste in the manner of their living. For when the man that we brought back to England on the last voyage would change his clothes, or even take off his coat, he would not permit the woman to be present but would put her out of the cabin. In the two or three months that the man and woman shared the same cabin, we saw nothing that we would not have seen had they been brother and sister. Still, the woman was very solicitous of the man, attending him carefully when he was sick. And similarly, when he was carving the meat they were to eat together, he would give her the sweetest, fattest, and best morsels they had. When we got back to England, they were amazed at everything they saw and were terrified of our horses and other animals. At the same time, they soon became more civil, familiar, pleasant, and docile.

They have boats made of leather that are completely covered except for one place in the middle to sit in. The boats are planked on the inside with timber, and are rowed a great deal more swiftly with one oar than ours are with twenty. They also have a larger kind of boat that can carry more than twenty people. It is fitted with a mast, and a sail made of thin skins and bladders sewn together with the sinews of fish.

They are good fishermen, and in their small boats, and disguised with their sealskin coats, they deceive the fish, who take them for fellow seals rather than deceiving men.

With their darts or arrows they are such good marksmen that they will commonly shoot ducks or any other birds in the head, and often in the eye.

When they shoot one of their darts at a great fish, they tie a bladder to the dart so that they can keep track of it more easily. In addition, the fish will not be able to escape so readily, because with the bladder buoying up the dart, it will at length become weary and die.

They trade with some other people for such things as their miserable country does not provide and their own ignorance of art prevents them from making. They receive in this trade such things as bars of iron, iron dart heads, square needles, and certain copper buttons which they wear upon their foreheads as ornaments, much as the ladies at the English court wear great pearls.

Using signs, they also told us that they had seen gold and bright metal plates which were used as ornaments among some people with whom they trade. And we found a red guinea bean, such as grows in the hot countries, in one of their tents; this suggests that they trade with some very distant nations, or else that they are great travellers.

They have no fuel for their fires except a kind of heath and moss that grows there. And they kindle their fire by continually rubbing and fretting one stick against another, as we do with flints. In summer, when they go hunting, they haul their tents on sleds, which they pull across the ice with their dogs. Occasionally they parboil their meat a little, seething it in skin kettles; they also have pans that are very skilfully made of stone. Fowl they take in crafty snares. The women carry their nursing infants at their backs and feed them raw meat, which they soften a little by chewing it in their own mouths.

The faces of the women are marked or painted over with small blue dots; and they have long, black hair which they keep decently trimmed. The men have but little hair on their faces, and very thin beards. For their common drink, they eat ice to quench their thirst. Their earth yields no grain or fruit for the sustenance of man and very little forage for animals. The natives eat grass and shrubs from the ground, even as our cattle do. Although no wood grows in their country, we find that they do have timber. This, we believe, grows far to the southward, probably in Canada or some other part of the new found land. There the trees are heavily weighted with snow and ice all winter; and then, when the ground thaws in the spring, those that stand on the cliffs are undermined by the waves and fall into the sea. Carried to and fro by the tides and currents, they are finally scattered along far-off beaches, where they are gathered up by these natives. They use them to plank and strengthen their boats, and to make spears, bows and arrows, and other things that they need. We find this kind of drift-wood all over the seas. It has been sawed or chopped, and through drifting in the water for a long time is full of worm-holes. This is the kind of wood that we found among the natives of Meta Incognita.

We have not yet found a venomous serpent or other dangerous creature in these parts; but there is a kind of small fly or gnat that offends very sorely, leaving many red spots on the face and other places where it bites. They have snow and hail in the middle of the summer, while the ground is frozen three fathom deep.

These people are great magicians, using many charms of witchcraft. When they have a headache, for example, they select a stone so heavy that a man cannot move it, and tie it to a stick with a piece of string. Then, after chanting certain words and prayers over the stick, they lift up the stone as though it were a feather, and hope to effect a cure with certain ceremonious words. Sometimes they lie with their faces abjectly in the dirt; we understood that when they utter a sound in this position, they are worshipping the Devil beneath them.

They have in their country a vast number of deer, bears, hares, and foxes, and incredible numbers of birds such as seamews, gulls, wilmots, ducks, etc., of which our men killed 1,500 in one day. They also have a number of hawks such as falcons, tassels, etc. On the return voyage, two of these alighted on one of the ships and were brought back to England. In addition, there is a great number of ravens, larks, and partridges, which the native peoples eat. All of these birds have thicker skins and are more heavily clothed with down and feathers than the birds in England. Thus, as the weather in that country is colder, nature has provided a remedy. Because their skins are so thick, these fowl must all be flayed; and they taste best when they are fried. Our men have eaten their bears, hares, partridges, larks, and other birds and find them reasonably good, but not so delectable as ours.

The country seems to be very subject to earthquakes. The air is very subtle, piercing, and searching, so that if any corrupted or in-fected person go there—especially with the disease called *Morbus Gallicus*[4]—it will presently break out. And it cannot be cured with any kind of salve or medicine so long as he stays in that country.

Their longest summer day is of great length and without any night, so that we could clearly and easily read or write anything we wished at any time. We found this very helpful when we were distressed with such an abundance of ice.

[4]Syphilis

The sun sets there at a quarter past ten at night and rises again at a quarter to two in the morning, so that it shines twenty hours and a half for them and is absent only three hours and a half. Although the sun is absent those three and a half hours, it is still not dark, for the sun is never more than three or four degrees below their horizon. This is because the tropic of Cancer cuts their horizon at very uneven and oblique angles. But any time of year that the moon is in Cancer and has north latitude, it makes a complete revolution above their horizon, so that they can sometimes see the moon for more than twenty-four hours at a stretch. Some of the more ignorant men thought that we might have seen both the sun and moon continually had it not been for three or four high mountains.

Because of their former losses, the natives have now grown so wary and circumspect that there is no way we can capture any of them, although we tried many times during the last voyage. But to tell the truth, we were so busy with our mining and other things that we could not devote much time to chasing them.

In conclusion, I found nothing in that entire country that was either pleasant or profitable, except what we dug out of the ground. There we found gold, silver, steel, iron, and black lead, together with very fine blue sapphires, which may encourage other men to further effort. And there is no doubt that when the land is examined more closely and is thoroughly explored, it will make our country both rich and exalted. And from these prosperous beginnings may we be granted happy endings by the goodness of God, to whom be all praise and glory. Amen.

1974

"Frobisher IV"

All is not golde that shineth.

George Best, 1578

1974

"Frobisher IV"

In August 1576, when Martin Frobisher returned from his first voyage to what is now the Canadian arctic, he brought with him what the Elizabethans referred to as "tokens of possession". These were objects that he had picked up and brought home as tangible proof that he had indeed visited some exotic land. Frobisher's tokens of possession were impeccable—an Eskimo with his kayak. No one in England had ever seen the like before, and during the short while that he remained alive in his new surroundings, people flocked from far and wide to see him.

Michael Lok was almost certainly among the first people in London to inspect this new curiosity. And he probably shared in the general amazement at the strange, fur-clad figure with the peculiar boat. But he expressed far greater interest in a rock which Frobisher gave him, a rock which one of the sailors had picked up on Hall's Islet, far to the northwest. It was a black rock, "which by waight seemed to be some kinde of metall or mynerall", according to a contemporary account. Lok's interest in this rock was more than academic, for he had invested some £800 of his own money in the search for the northwest passage, and so far had nothing to show for it but Frobisher's assurance that the entrance to that passage had been found. However, if that heavy black rock should prove to be some kind of ore, if it were to contain gold or some other valuable mineral, then his investment would be amply repaid. So Lok set forth in search of an assayer.

The first few assayers whom Lok approached told him frankly that the rock was worthless. He persisted, however, till he finally found one who knew how to "flatter nature", as he put it, and who conveniently reported that the sample did indeed contain gold. The obliging assayer—or goldfiner, as he was called in those days—was a persuasive Italian alchemist named John Baptista Agnello. He convinced Lok that his assessment of the ore was accurate, although he could not convince Lok's fellow venturers. These insisted on calling in independent experts, who invariably reported that the ore was worthless. However, Lok's opinion ultimately prevailed, and the second expedition to the northwest was launched, but only after Lok had agreed to underwrite most of the costs of the new venture himself. Spurred on by a delicate blend of hope and cupidity, Lok and his associates brought back some 2,000 tons of rock over the next two years. But by the end of the third voyage, in the fall of 1578, it was obvious that the whole thing had been a hoax. There simply was no gold.

The story of Martin Frobisher and his search for a northwest passage is woven into the very fabric of our history. But what of the rock that Michael Lok carried so hopefully from one assayer to another? It is now almost 400 years since Frobisher's men first hefted a chunk of that black rock and decided that it must be some kind of "metall or mynerall"; and through all that time it has been assumed that the rock which Frobisher collected must have been some form of iron pyrites. But no one really knew, because none of Frobisher's ore has survived.

A few years ago, the Royal Ontario Museum decided that the 400th anniversary of Frobisher's first voyage should not be allowed to pass unnoticed. For that 1576 voyage was the earliest attempt to sail around the northern end of the newly discovered continent, rather than through it, as earlier explorers had hoped to do. Although Frobisher's "straits" proved to be nothing more than a bay, and his "gold mines" proved to be worthless, yet his voyages cannot be looked upon as complete failures. For they bequeathed to us our earliest description of what is now the Canadian arctic, as well as providing our introduction to the people who lived there—the Eskimo. In preparation for the anniversary celebrations, therefore, I decided to visit Baffin Island, and particularly Kodlunarn Island in Countess of Warwick Sound, where Frobisher had mined much of the ore that he brought back on his third voyage. We would measure and photograph his mines and collect samples of the rock from the trenches that Frobisher's men had dug so long ago, and which Charles Francis Hall had located and described in 1861–62.

My first view of Baffin Island was from a Nordair Jet out of Montreal in the late summer of 1973. As we approached the island's southern shore, the waters of Hudson Strait below us were garnished with a scattering of pale, greenish-white icebergs that looked like bleached-out emeralds against a swatch of dark blue velvet. The Island itself rose before us in a series of swirls that resembled some gigantic marble cake. In the folds and creases in the surface of the bare rock were patches of snow and ice left over from the blizzards of the previous winter. Before I left for Frobisher Bay, I had arranged to charter a small plane on floats to take me down the bay as far as Countess of

The Grinnell Glacier from the air

Warwick Sound, but I discovered at the last minute that it was not available. There was a Twin Otter standing by, however, and so I decided to charter that. I was rather annoyed to discover that the Otter was on wheels rather than floats, because that ruled out any possibility of landing in the bay. But I got the impression that the pilot did not share my enthusiasm for landing a small plane in Countess of Warwick Sound in any event.

What I needed at that point was some idea of the kind of archaeological problem that I would face when I arrived there the following summer with a crew. I needed that information so that I could select a crew and draw up an equipment list that bore some reasonable relationship to the work that I would have to do. Ideally, I should have examined the area in some detail, or at least have selected a camp site and located a source of drinking water. But as that was not possible, I had to be satisfied with what I could learn through an aerial reconnaissance. Cruising down the bay at about 3,000 feet, we had perfect visibility under a pale blue and cloudless sky. I had already told the pilot that I would want to drop down for some low-level photography when we reached Countess of Warwick Sound, down near Davis Strait. Meanwhile, I just sat there watching the scenery go by—the Grinnell Glacier capping Meta Incognita on our right, slabs of ice drifting about in the bay below us, and away to the north, a high, snow-covered plateau. The whole thing was magnificent.

Far to the east, meanwhile, a dense ground-fog was moving across Baffin Island from Davis Strait, blotting out everything but the highest peaks and plateaus. When the pilot saw that the fog was rolling into Countess of Warwick Sound while we were still many miles away, he called me forward for instructions. There was obviously no point in continuing on our planned course, so I diverted the flight to the south shore of Frobisher Bay, where the Grinnell Glacier was glistening in the sun. As we swung in a wide circle across the bay, we saw that the cliffs on the south shore rose abruptly from the water, soaring in places to a height of over 1,000 feet. The entire shoreline had a serrated edge, being cut by a series of sounds, bays, and valleys, in a few of which long white ribbons of ice swept down from the glacier on the highlands to the water's edge below. Looking at a topographic map of the area, I could see that the north side of the bay was neither so rugged nor so lofty as the magnificent south shore that we were now following back to the town of Frobisher Bay. But the north shore, too, was obviously rugged in some places, and one of the places was Countess of Warwick Sound, where the Harris Highlands rose almost vertically to a height of some 1,200 feet. I ought really to have seen that sound before moving in with a crew, and I thought of lying over at the Frobisher Inn till the weather cleared. But what could I see from the air that I had not already seen? Very little, in all probability. So I decided to return to Toronto, and play the next passage by ear.

Back at the office, I tried to figure out what size of crew I would need, and how long we could conveniently hope to spend in Countess of Warwick Sound. The latter problem was solved by the government records of ice and weather conditions in Frobisher Bay and Davis Strait. According to these, it would probably be impossible for us to get down the bay in a small boat until very late in July; and by early September the weather would probably be so bad that we should no longer be able to accomplish anything. That is, I could expect reasonably good weather—or what passes for good weather in that part of the world—only during the month of August. I decided, therefore, to get in and out in three weeks, if that were at all possible.

Selecting a crew for the Frobisher Expedition was a bit complicated because I was unable to convert our archaeological objectives into specific tasks. And this I should have done, so that I could select people with the necessary skills for performing them. However, it was fairly clear that a crew of eight people should be able to handle any problem that might come up. Eight was also the largest number of people that I could take along without running into administrative or logistical diffi-

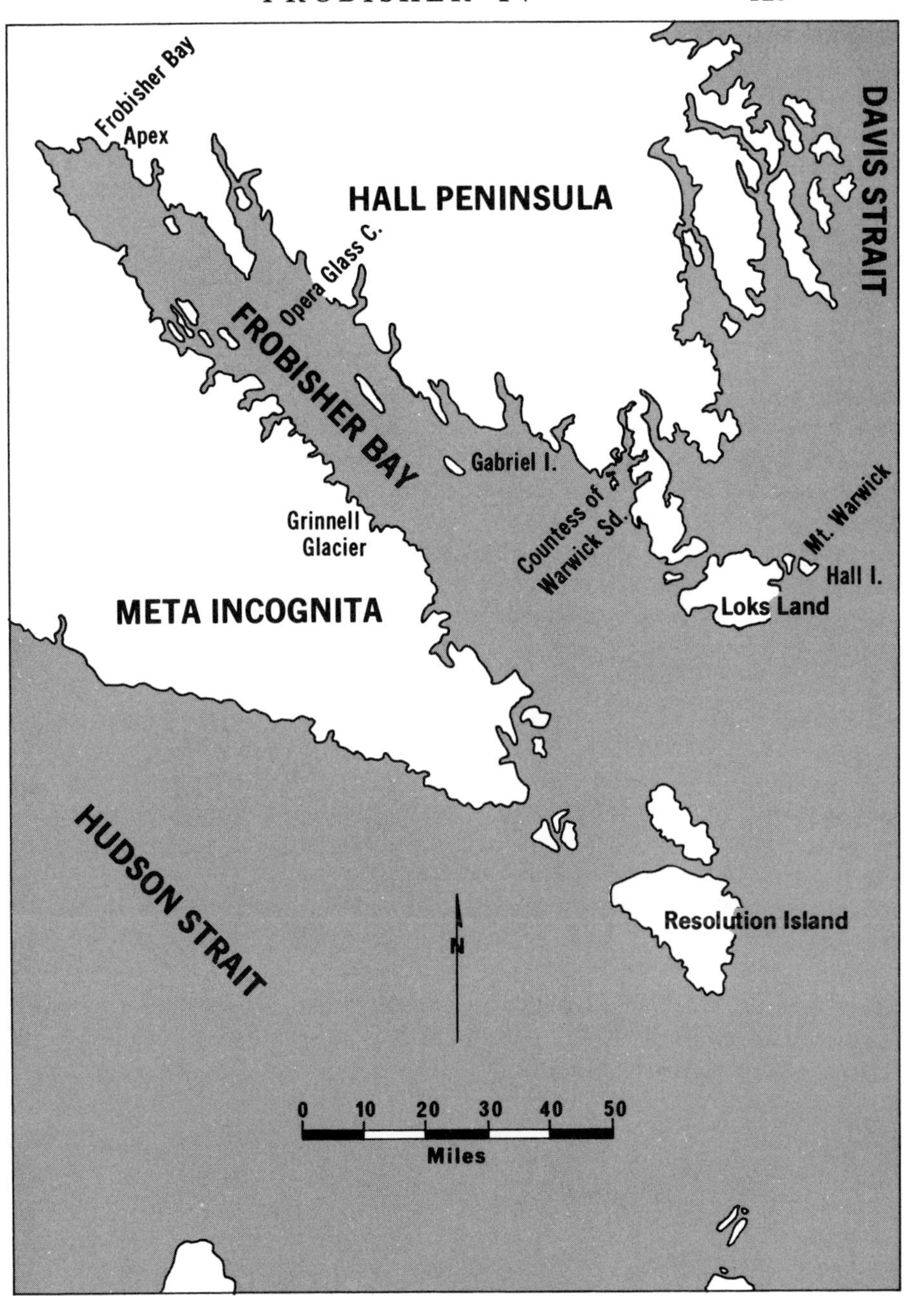

Frobisher Bay

culties. So eight it would be. What I needed was a few people with broad archaeological experience, and a couple of men who could handle freight canoes in rough water and cope with tides that might approach twenty-five feet in height. And all of them must have demonstrated their ability to live and work under severely adverse conditions.

Fortunately, there were a few experienced northerners around, people who had worked with me on other projects in places such as James Bay. From these I selected Jim Sheppard of Sudbury and Dave Lightwood of Moosonee as boatmen and general assistants. I needed someone with academic training in historic archaeology, and after discussing the problem with my colleagues in the Department of Anthropology at Trent University, I hired Judy Marsh, one of their students from Cobourg. Irene Dawson from London and John Chambers from Hamilton were both experienced northerners, and were fortunately both available. Michael Lee, my laboratory and field assistant from the Museum, probably feels by now that I could not survive in the north without his help; as I have the uneasy feeling that he might be right, I added him to the list. The final member of the group was my daughter, Diane, who is another experienced northerner. As I checked over the crew list, I felt that we could probably handle any archaeological problem that we were likely to encounter, and so I put that list aside and started drawing up equipment lists and schedules, a task which kept me occupied throughout much of the following winter.

We left Toronto at 5:00 a.m. on Tuesday, July 30, 1974, carrying all of our personal gear, as well as the cameras, film, and a surveyor's transit. At Montreal we changed from Air Canada to Nordair, and flew to Frobisher Bay in a Boeing 737, arriving at 12:30 p.m. We were met at the airport by Bill McKenzie, a northern outfitter who was supplying us with such things as tents, stoves, wheelbarrows, and planks, and who had assembled and packed the groceries that I had ordered by mail. He had also chartered a boat and two twenty-foot freight canoes to take us down the bay to Countess of Warwick Sound. Bill told us that the vessel was fogged in a few miles down the bay, but should be back the next day. Meanwhile, he loaded our gear onto a truck and drove us to Apex, a small village about three miles east of Frobisher Bay, where he kindly installed us in his own home to wait for the weather to clear.

The next day, July 31, the entire island from Hudson Strait to Pond Inlet was blanketed with fog, and it was not till almost six o'clock the following evening that the vessel dropped its anchor off the beach at Apex. It was a beautiful, white, forty-four-foot long-liner which, like

The long-liner

all the other boats which I saw at Frobisher Bay, had no name. It had
a tiny forecastle with a sink, a Coleman stove, and three bunks with
folded caribou skins for mattresses. The skins were not tanned or
smoked, but merely dried, with bits of raw, dried meat still adhering
to them. The wheelhouse was aft, and there was a small hold amid-
ships. Another bunk, they told me, was located in the hold on the
starboard side.

We finally got under way about 10:30 p.m. on August 1. When I
counted the crew, I discovered that we had six Eskimo aboard; these
were the captain, Pootaliq, the chief engineer, Joanasee, and the deck-
hand, Frank, as well as three others. One of the others was an older
man, Mosesee, who I gathered was Joanasee's uncle, and who seemed
to be acting as pilot because he knew where the rocks were in the
lower part of the bay. The other two never were identified. With all
our gear and fourteen people aboard, we barely had room to move
about. The three girls, Michael, and John managed to cram themselves
into the forecastle, while the rest of us stayed on deck, wedged in between piles of tents and wheelbarrows, drums of diesel fuel, mixed gas
for the outboard motors, naphtha gas for Coleman stoves and lanterns,
and coal oil for the primus stoves.

Finally, with everything in order, more or less, we weighed anchor and headed down the bay at about eight knots. No one actually knew how fast we were going, and no one really seemed interested in such a purely academic question, for ours was apparently a very casual ship. A large compass was gimballed into a free-standing wooden box that sat on a shelf in front of the helmsman. He paid no attention to it, however, shoving it aside if it got in the way of the stove he used for making tea. I suspect that the compass, like the single life-preserver aboard, was simply to give the vessel a nautical appearance. In any event, most of the older Eskimo seemed to know every rock, reef, and island in Frobisher Bay, as it turned out. Although there was almost solid overcast (I saw but a single star all night) there was plenty of light to work the vessel through the maze of reefs and shoals scattered across the entire upper bay. Blobs of ice, rarely more than thirty feet across, had to be avoided also, but these were easy to detect because they glowed in the dark with a pale, unblinking light. Once the town of Frobisher Bay had disappeared astern, our isolation from the rest of the world was complete. I spent most of the night on deck, watching the islands and cakes of ice drift slowly past.

About two o'clock in the morning, I noticed a light patch in the overcast and thought that the cloud cover was starting to break up. I realized after watching it for some time that it was not a break in the overcast at all, but the iceblink of the Grinnell Glacier. I remained on deck till I could no longer stay awake, then hauled some of the gear out of the hold, searching for the bunk that they told me was down there. When I found it, it was just the length of a modest-sized archae-ologist, and rather narrower. There was barely enough space to wedge myself and my claustrophobia onto the narrow shelf, where I slept on my back with my face just a few inches from the deck beams. After sleeping for an hour or so, I crawled out on deck to drink some scalding hot tea and eat a couple of bully-beef sandwiches. Jim and Dave were sound asleep under a tarpaulin on deck; the rest of my crew were sleep-ing in the forecastle, wedged into all manner of odd nooks and crannies.

Although he was very small and looked extremely frail, I soon dis-covered that Mosesee was actually a very tough old bird. After being at the wheel most of the night, he went forward at dawn—that is, about 3:30 a.m.—and crawled under a tarpaulin lying on the port side of the hatch to have a nap. I knew nothing of all this, as I was in the forecastle at the time, drinking a cup of tea. When I came up on deck, I walked across the tarpaulin on my way aft, as I had been doing all night. Only when I stepped on something soft did I realize that there was a small

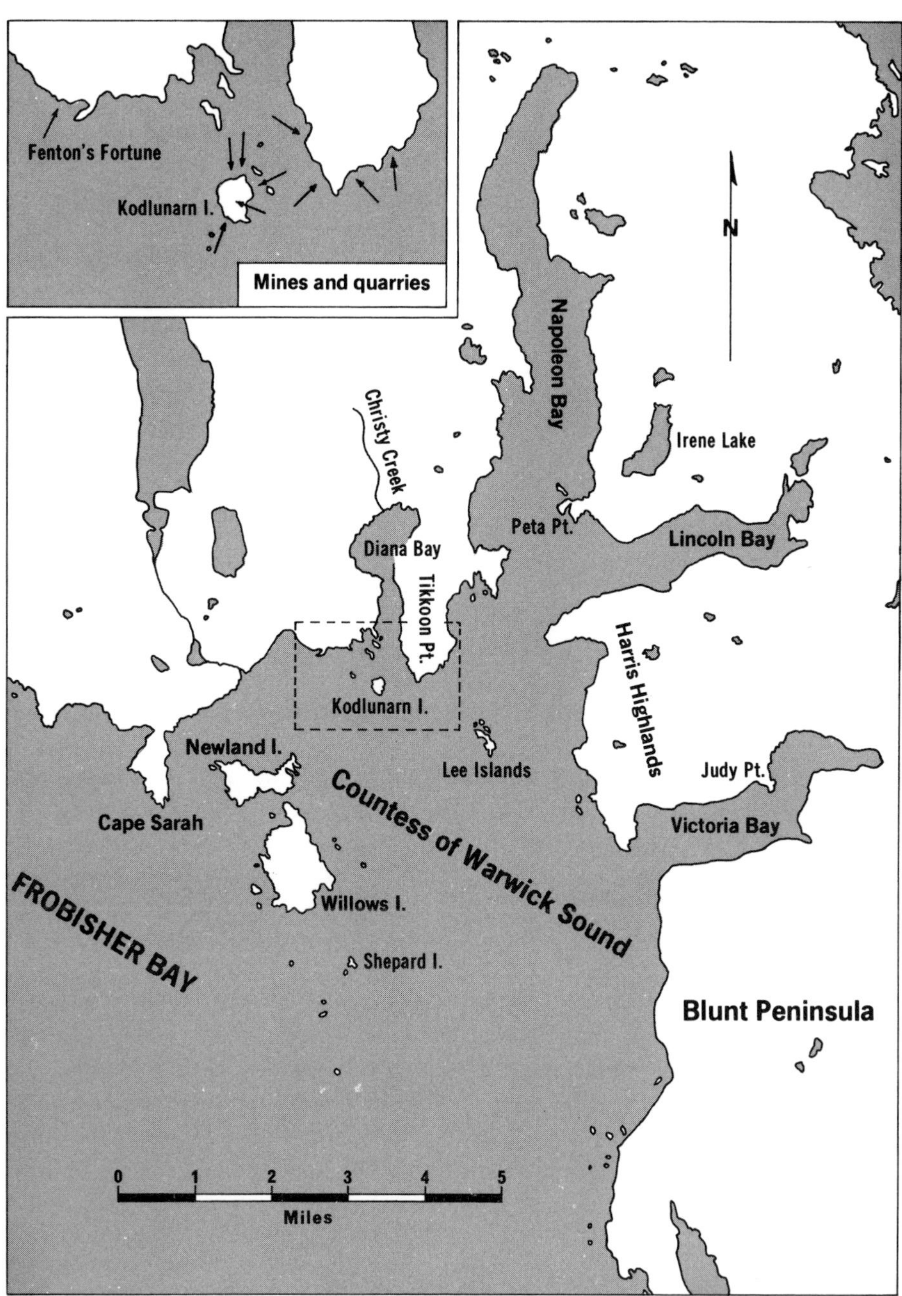

Countess of Warwick Sound

lump of some yielding material between the canvas and the deck. A hand slowly emerged and folded back a flap of canvas; the face of Mosesee smiled up at me, then, like some ancient and benevolent tortoise, was slowly drawn back under its protective shell. Muttering an apology, I continued aft.

As the crew members woke up, we stuffed each one with cups of sweet, scalding hot tea and corned-beef sandwiches. Everyone except the natives seemed to be suffering from lack of sleep, and from sore, stiff muscles as a result of having been packed so tightly into awkward and improbable positions. Early that morning, I stopped noting the time at which anything happened, as it no longer seemed important. At one point, we shot and harpooned a young harp seal; at another, we went into a maze of narrow, twisted channels near the head of Gabriel Island to pick up a drum of diesel fuel that was cached there. Just before we reached Countess of Warwick Sound, Mike pointed to a small island and said "polar bear". There was a brief chase, but it was abandoned when the bear took to the water and headed for another island.

Continuing down the north shore of the bay, we entered Countess of Warwick Sound through the narrow channel between Newland Island and Cape Sarah at 4:30 p.m. After an eighteen-hour run in a small, cramped boat, we were all exhausted. I did no more than glance at Kodlunarn Island as we passed that low, small, unimposing feature. I asked the captain to take us to any camp site that was close to the island and that had a reasonably good supply of drinking water. He took us to Tikkoon Point, which is separated from Kodlunarn Island by a narrow channel only a few hundred yards wide. As I walked ashore, I noticed some old tent-rings and a scattering of seal, walrus, and caribou bones. The site was in a low pass running across a point which was only about 100 yards wide, and protected on the north by a steep slope, still covered with snow.

The next day, August 3, was solidly overcast, with a northwest wind and occasional rain. We spent the day putting our camp in order—digging an outhouse, lining a small pool with rocks so that we could get clear drinking water, making sure that the grub and the gear would not get wet if the tents leaked, and similar chores. Together with trying to keep moderately warm and dry, these tasks kept us fully occupied all day. When we finally crawled into our sleeping bags, the wind had increased markedly and the showers were becoming heavier. I slept fitfully, expecting during each lull that the next gust would surely flatten my tent. Finally, when I could stand it no longer, I got up and brewed a pot of coffee. As I stood there shivering at 3:30 in the morning, I swore a solemn oath that I would never again go into the field without being absolutely certain that I was properly equipped.

All that day, August 4, the wind blew, pounding the rain against our soggy tents. The quantity of rain that actually fell was probably not very great, but the gusting wind drove it against us with disconcerting force. Every time one of the crew touched the inside of a tent, a small trickle of water would pour through the violated spot. I watched apprehensively for the tents to collapse, but miraculously they remained standing. Our kitchen and dining room was a large tarpaulin held aloft, more or less, by some stray bits and pieces of lumber that we had picked up at Frobisher Bay. The south end was largely blocked by a rock outcrop, but the north end was open, so we closed it off by draping groundsheets and gunny-sacks across the opening. The east and west sides of the structure were simply weighted down with large rocks. Inside, we had a half sheet of plywood supported by four ten-gallon gas drums for a table. It was a very cold and dismal place.

The camp at Tikkoon Point

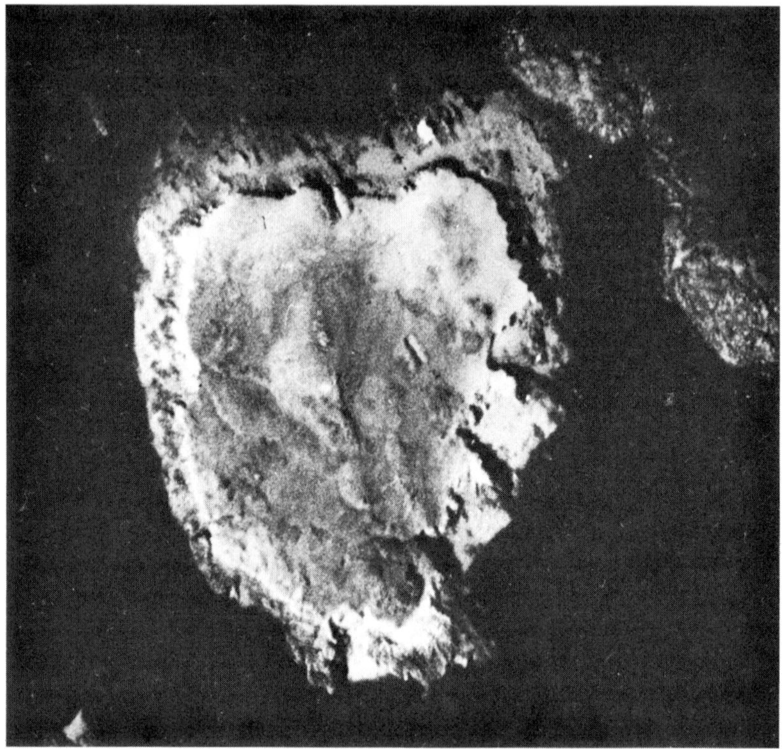

Aerial photo of Kodlunarn Island. Both the "ship's trench" and the "reservoir or mine" are clearly visible. Original photograph supplied by the National Air Photo Library, Department of Energy, Mines and Resources.

The next night was just as bad. I spent most of it waiting for my tent to blow down, with high winds, gusting from the east, threatening to flatten it at any moment. When morning came, I learned that two of the tents had gone down in the night but had been put up again; they were all throughly soaked, however, and so the crew had doubled up in the ones that were comparatively dry for the rest of the night. Once again we huddled together in the kitchen tent, with two Coleman stoves going full blast, in the vain hope that we could eventually dry ourselves out. From time to time, however, I would wander out of the tent to stand in the rain, gazing wistfully across to Kodlunarn Island.

It was 396 years ago, almost to the day, that Frobisher's fleet had sailed for the last time from its anchorage off that island. Since then, it had been visited on only two occasions by scientific parties that had any interest in Frobisher. The first of these was the visit of Charles

Charles Francis Hall's map of Kodlunarn Island. Redrawn from Charles Francis Hall, *Life with the Esquimaux* (London: Sampson Low, Son, and Marston, 1864).

Francis Hall, who landed on Kodlunarn Island on September 21, 1861. It was Hall who first heard from the Eskimo of southeastern Baffin Island the incredible tale of some white men who had visited the area a great many years earlier. As he collected more and more details of those early visits, he realized that the Eskimo must have been talking about the voyages of Martin Frobisher, and that the story must have been handed down orally from generation to generation through 282 years. Oddly enough, through all that time—almost three centuries—the only people in the world who knew where Frobisher had been in his search for the northwest passage were a handful of Eskimo who had never heard his name. Realizing the importance of his discovery, Hall gathered up a few relics which he found strewn about the island, surveyed it quickly but accurately, and drew a map which he published in his *Life with the Esquimaux*. His map shows the locations of Best's Bulwark and the ruins of a small house, both of which are mentioned in the Frobisher journals. It also shows two large excavations, which Hall called a "ship's trench or mine" and a "reservoir or mine", as well as the ruins of a shop. The only other party to visit Kodlunarn Island was the Rawson-MacMillan Sub-Arctic Expedition in 1927. The members of that party spent only a few hours on the island, just long enough to confirm Hall's report.

At last, as I stood outside the tent peering through the drizzle, I convinced myself that the weather was actually improving. True, it was still raining, but as I pointed out to the crew, it did seem to be getting lighter, and if we were to head for Kodlunarn Island immediately, it would almost certainly have cleared up by the time we got there. Climbing into the canoe, we swung around to the north side of the island because there were some reefs just off the eastern edge of the island, the side that we were facing. Oddly enough, it seemed to be raining harder when we reached the island and climbed up a steep rubble slope to its relatively flat surface. Because of the rain on my glasses I could not see very much, but the crew scurried about and quickly located the major features that had been reported by Charles Francis Hall 113 years earlier. Nothing, apparently, had changed. By this time, everyone was thoroughly drenched, so we headed back to camp.

We slept till almost 8:00 o'clock the next morning, August 6, and woke up to a beautiful, clear day with just enough scattered cloud to lend variety to a sparkling blue sky. After a breakfast of bacon, scrambled eggs, fried potatoes, and coffee, we spread our gear out on the rocks to dry. Tents were re-rigged, and holes were punched in their floors to drain out the larger and deeper pools.

While the camp was drying out, I sent some of the crew over to the island to measure Frobisher's mines, and to see if their locations agreed with Hall's map. Meanwhile, Joanasee, Jim, and I went over to a point north of Kodlunarn Island where Mosesee told me there were some old winter houses. We found a number of them scattered along the beach and named the place "Native Point".

In the afternoon, I took the long-liner up into Napoleon Bay to see what was there. It was a beautiful, deep fjord running a few miles inland, with high, eroded cliffs and hills on each side. On the way in, we spotted a caribou standing on a low ridge, clearly outlined against the pale blue sky. Two or three rifles banged away, and the caribou disappeared over the ridge. The big boat was then nosed quickly ashore—we had no tender—and a couple of the men climbed out on the rocks. As we backed off and swung the boat around, there were two shots in rapid succession, and presently we saw the caribou swimming in the water. As we slid the boat in between the caribou and the shore I saw that it had been wounded; the hunters waited till I had taken a few pictures, and then quickly dispatched it. Seconds later it had been caught with a boat hook, hauled aboard, skinned, dressed, and cut up. When we returned to camp, Joanasee asked if we would like some of the meat, and being told that we would, he put a haunch—perhaps 30 lb. of meat—into a cardboard carton for us, and we buried it in the snowbank behind our camp.

In our wanderings about, we had picked up stray pieces of rock which we carried back to camp for closer examination. Apart from the occasional bit of quartz, mica, or magnetite, our rock collection consisted of three basic rocks. First, there was a black rock that must have been the material that Frobisher's men referred to as the "black ore". Next there was what appeared to be a metamorphic rock of some kind composed of thin strata. Most of the strata were some shade of pink, though these alternated occasionally with strata of various shades of gray. From a distance, this material was a light pink, although it actually exhibited a wide variation in colour when examined closely. This must have been the "red ore" of Frobisher's miners. The third basic rock in our collection was pegmatite.

Kodlunarn Island seemed to be composed of the black and reddish rocks, cut occasionally by a pegmatite dike. In fact, the whole southeastern corner of Baffin Island appeared to be composed of the same material that Frobisher was mining. Why, then, did Frobisher dig out "ore" from one place rather than another? Having decided that I needed to see more of the country before I could hope to answer that question, I started exploring. While half the crew remained to continue the measuring and mapping on Kodlunarn, I took the other half up Napoleon Bay to the spot where Lincoln Bay branches off to the right. Anchoring the long-liner behind Peta Point, we explored an old Eskimo camp there and picked up a few interesting magnetite crystals. Then a couple of us took a canoe up into Lincoln Bay, while some of the Eskimo walked up the valley to Irene Lake before scattering across the surrounding hills in search of caribou.

Lincoln Bay is a narrow fjord, with steep cliffs rising from the water's edge to a height of about 1,200 feet. At the end of the bay is a large clear patch of snow that looks as if it might have been imported from some alpine valley. At the foot of the cliffs, the water is a dark bluish-green. Without trees to use as a scale, I doubted very much that my camera would capture the brooding immensity of a

Lincoln Bay

place that was either magnificent or terrifying, depending on your point of view.

After returning to the long-liner and collecting our hunters, we moved south to Victoria Bay, another deep, spectacular fjord. The only flat spot in the bay is a small, low point of land jutting out into the bay from the north side. This must be the place where Charles Francis Hall reported finding a deposit of coal.

While we were turning around at the very end of the bay, there was a blast of gunfire as someone spotted a seal. Joanasee, who was at the helm, followed the seal westward along the south shore of the bay till it was finally killed. When it was hauled out to the long-liner by one of the canoes, I discovered that it was not just another harp seal, but a huge square-flipper that must have weighed 400 lb. The men had a three-quarter-inch manila rope rigged to a small boom for heaving heavy objects aboard; to this they attached a length of heavy walrus-hide line, which they threaded through a cut in the seal's mandible, then looped around his snout. They had winched the seal about half way out of the water when there was a loud crack as the mandible split, and the seal disappeared into the black water. Apart from myself, no one seemed particularly upset. As we headed back to camp, I continued examining the cliffs and talus slopes through binoculars; they all appeared to consist of the same rocks that Frobisher had been mining on Kodlunarn Island.

I was continually amazed at the number of people scattered around Countess of Warwick Sound. Each time the men returned from a hunting trip, there seemed to be a new man aboard. And almost every day a strange canoe would appear from some bay or cove, scurry across the water, and then disappear into a neighbouring bay, or perhaps behind some island. If I had not known better, I would probably have concluded that the Eskimo were generated by spontaneous combustion behind isolated rocks, or deep in the clefts of nameless harbours. The truth, as always, was more mundane. There were a number of Eskimo families that were spending their holidays in the area. Many of the natives of Frobisher Bay move down there for a couple of weeks in the summer, in the same way that residents of Toronto will head for Muskoka or Wasaga Beach for their holidays.

It amazed me, also, to find out what a detailed knowledge of the area most of the natives have. Of the six men on our boat, four could take me to any bay, cove, or island in Frobisher Bay; and three of them could take me to Lake Harbour, Cape Dorset, or Pangnirtung as well. One night while I was showing the men a nautical chart, I pointed to Christopher Hall Island in Davis Strait, where I hoped to go later on. They nodded calmly, then told me that there was a high rock cairn on top of a hill there. I had always thought of Mount Warwick as that incredibly remote spot climbed and named by Martin Frobisher 400 years ago when he built the cairn. The combination of extreme isolation and historic associations made it almost a sacred place. To me, Mount Warwick and Mount Olympus were in the same class—different, certainly, but sharing certain qualities that set them apart from more common mountains. To the Eskimo, on the other hand, Mount Warwick is just another hill, and it's not remote at all, it's just beyond that big island.

During my explorations, I always tried to take one or two of the crew with me, leaving the others to continue the work on Kodlunarn Island. The exploration was important because that was the only way we could develop the broader perspective we would need to interpret our archaeological data. Meanwhile, of course, we had to continue the clearing, mapping, and description of the historic clues that Frobisher's men had left on Kodlunarn Island.

Seen from our camp, Kodlunarn was a flat-topped island with some low ridges and outcrops, but with a very sharp and vertical edge above the tidal zone. From the normal high-tide line, that edge rose some twenty-one feet. The highest point on the island was found to be a rock outcrop, just to the east of Frobisher's house, that measured sixty-one feet above the high-tide line; the foundation of the house itself was fifty-seven feet above the same mark.

A line measured from the mouth of the "ship's trench", through the "reservoir or mine", to the edge of the bank in the cove south of Best's Bulwark was 684 feet long.

The "ship's trench" was cut into the island from the north side, with the back-dirt thrown up into what is now a rounded ridge on both sides of the trench. The trench itself measured 80 feet in length.

View of Kodlunarn Island from the camp

The "ship's trench", from the landward end

The "ship's trench", seen from the sea

The "reservoir or mine"

Where it cut the vertical bank at the edge of the island, it was 10 feet deep and 28 feet wide. From there, the floor of the trench sloped upward to the surface of the island where it had tapered to a width of 13 feet.

The depression that Charles Francis Hall called a "reservoir or mine" was 88 feet long, with roughly parallel sides and rounded ends. It was 5 feet deep, and 20 feet wide at the widest point. That is, the trench was a flattened oval, and it was surrounded by a pile of back-dirt some 30 to 40 inches high.

On the morning of August 11, we woke up to a soft, purple haze that had reduced visibility to about a mile. My judgment of distances there in the sound was still very poor, so that I could not tell the difference between a 100-foot cliff one mile away, and a 1,000-foot cliff 10 miles away. When the distance became important, I checked it on the map. Most of the time, however, I was content simply to look and admire, for the colours constantly changed with the time of day, and with what was probably the moisture content of the air. I was not sure what caused it, but on occasion there would be a straggle of icebergs down at the mouth of the bay. Then, for no reason that I could figure out, they would disappear. I knew they were still there, for there was one monstrously large berg that was grounded far down the bay and had not changed its position during all the time we had been there. But it was only visible occasionally, and so I deduced that

Davis Strait was usually hidden behind an invisible optical screen. It was all very mysterious and lovely.

After breakfast, I went over to Native Point with Jim and Judy to examine the old Eskimo settlement. We located some fourteen or fifteen winter houses there, and I noticed that since my previous visit to the site about a week earlier, most of the houses had been very superficially dug into. I suspect that our talk about Frobisher's gold mines had reverberated through the Eskimo community, and they were after a piece of the action. The site there, like the saddleback in which we were camped, was littered with bones, mostly walrus and seal.

While Judy and Jim were mapping one of the houses, I strolled to the west along a low ridge, parallel to the shore. Looking back at one point, I saw in the wall of a tiny inlet what appeared to be a cave. Returning to investigate it, I saw what was clearly a man-made cut into the rock. It was cut into the same red rock that Frobisher's men had been hand-spiking off the cliffs on Kodlunarn Island. I did not have a tape measure with me long enough to measure the height of the rock face into which the mine had been cut. We would have to return later to measure and record that new feature. I did examine the whole area rather closely, however, as I was struck with the quantity of broken rock that was lying about. For I had recently observed that deposits of broken rocks that exhibited sharp, angular breaks were found only along the shore, and that such deposits seemed to occur only in association with the mining or quarrying activities of Frobisher's men.

When we got back to camp there were heavy black cloud banks to the east, west, and south of us; and just before going to bed I noticed that a bank of fog was sitting on top of the Harris Highlands, and was beginning to spill over the rims of both Lincoln and Victoria bays. Long wisps of cloud were hanging down the sides of the canyon like foam. When I woke up the next morning, August 12, a warm, gentle rain had washed out everything but the hill directly behind us and a few feet of shoreline. Apart from the falling rain, there was not a sound to be heard. Even the waves, instead of splashing gently against the rocks as they usually did, were silent. As I stood there soaking up the solitude, one of the girls in a nearby tent started to talk in her sleep. Feeling like an intruder, I coughed modestly as I went into the kitchen tent to heat water for coffee, leaving her to her maidenly dreams. After raining all day it finally stopped, but when I stepped outside the tent to look around, I could see nothing beyond the island, although I could see that quite clearly. It was solidly overcast, and there was not a breath of wind.

The next morning, August 13, we woke up to another wet, raw day. There was a modest wind gusting out of the east, but it was nothing like the storm we had had just after we arrived there. On a day like that, there was really nothing we could do except try to keep warm and dry. Oddly enough, that was a full-time occupation because of the tents we had. We had nine tents in camp at the time, in addition to the kitchen, but six of them were totally inadequate for that climate. They were wildly unstable in a high wind, and they leaked. After a few hours of rain, everything in them was damp, and there was really no way of drying them out.

A few days earlier, the Eskimo crew had taken the long-liner back to Frobisher Bay to pick up new supplies of diesel fuel and ammunition. Just before he left, Joanasee had come to me and asked if I would like another chunk of caribou meat. When I told him that I would, he sent one of the men back to the boat to pick it up. When the man returned, he was carrying a slab of meat that probably weighed 10 to 15 lb. The animal had been shot several days before, and after being cleaned and cut up, the pieces had simply been piled up on the short length of deck at the back corner of the wheelhouse. Exposed to the air, the meat had developed a dark, dry skin which was liberally peppered with stray caribou hairs. My crew knew that anyone going aft along the port side of the vessel was almost certain to step on that pile of meat if the vessel happened to lurch at the right time, as it usually did. Probably all fourteen of us had stepped on that pile of meat at one time or another.

The man who brought us the chunk of meat tossed it nonchalantly on a large flat rock in front of the kitchen tent. As I watched the crew examine it with obvious distaste, I wondered what their reaction would be if I suggested cooking it. When an opportunity presented itself, I asked them what they would prefer for lunch, caribou steaks or beans and bacon? The unanimous choice was beans. While lunch was being prepared, I quietly threw a couple of slabs of caribou meat into a frying pan, together with a few slices of bacon and a handful of chopped onions. Then, as the delicate aroma spread throughout the kitchen, one of the more daring members of the crew asked to try it and, finding it to his taste, prevailed on the others to try it also. They immediately became dedicated and enthusiastic caribou eaters. Before we returned to the bright lights of Frobisher Bay, we had eaten caribou steaks, braised caribou with beans, caribou stew with dumplings, sautéed caribou with bacon and onions, as well as curried caribou. And they were all delicious.

For three days, the bad weather continued. I stood around helplessly, hour after hour and day after day, watching the wind and the rain batter down my camp. Time after time the tents were re-rigged, but to little avail. They were just not built for the beating they were taking. As our physical situation deteriorated, anxiety levels rose sharply. No one said anything, but more and more time was spent on speculation as to when the vessel would return. It became increasingly obvious, therefore, that I would have to finish my work in Countess of Warwick Sound and head back to the town of Frobisher Bay within the next few days, and certainly before the next storm hit us, if that were at all possible. So I drew up a list of the most urgent things that remained to be done, then simply waited for the weather to clear up.

On Thursday, August 15, we woke up at 6:30 a.m. to a warm, sunny day, with a low, scattered overcast and a gentle breeze out of the west. As I looked around, it was hard to believe that the charming landscape spread out before me was actually the same place in which we had spent the previous three days. We dragged our soggy sleeping bags, clothes, and other gear out of the tents to dry, and cleaned up the kitchen. Some of the hardier souls even washed themselves. Then, after a hearty breakfast, we all went to the island, except for two of the crew whom I left in camp to keep an eye on the drying gear. On the island, we opened a small test trench in the cove north of Best's Bulwark where we had noticed a thin lens of coal eroding out of the

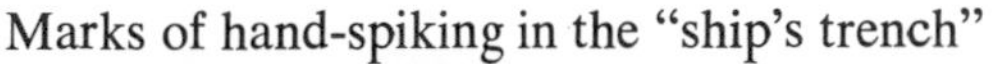

Marks of hand-spiking in the "ship's trench"

bank a few days earlier. Once the trench was started, I did a final examination of the "ship's trench", and verified my earlier impression that it had been quarried into the solid rock by hand-spiking or picking the strata apart.

After photographing Best's Bulwark and some of the spots where the pink rock had been quarried north of there, I went over to the cove to the west of Native Point to measure and photograph the mine we had found there a few days before. It was located towards the north end of a long, vertical rock face, with the floor of the cut just a few feet above the high-tide mark. The mine itself was 6½ feet wide, 13 feet high, and 10 feet deep. It cut through 4 feet of the pink rock, and then 6 feet of the black. The rock face itself was 22 feet high, and had been quarried off for its entire length, about 55 feet. In that area, the rock strata run approximately north and south, while the tops of the strata slope to the east at an angle of about 30° from the vertical.

By that time I had checked every one of Frobisher's rock-cuts that I could locate, and had not yet found one bit of lichen growing on any of them. On his back-dirt, on the other hand, the lichen was very thick in some areas, particularly on the south and west slopes. For some reason, it seemed to grow more readily on small rocks than on large slabs. Coarse gravel about cobblestone size seemed to promote the most luxuriant growth.

Apart from a very light haze in the distance, the next morning, August 16, was clear and sparkling. When I crawled out of the tent

Best's Bulwark

The mine near Native Point.
This was probably Fenton's
Fortune.

View to the east from Judy Point

at about 5:30, the long-liner was riding comfortably at anchor, and the enticing aroma of coffee, pancakes, and bacon was floating out of the kitchen. After breakfast, a few of us took the long-liner (with a native crew that now consisted of at least eight people) over to the point in Victoria Bay. Again, I was struck with the immensity of the cliffs and the impossibility of capturing that immensity on film. In an attempt to get some idea of the scale involved, I anchored the vessel against the north shore of the bay and photographed it from the point. The cliffs there were composed of a twisted and convoluted rock that rose steeply for some 1,200 feet to what appeared to be relatively flat plateaus. At the foot of the cliffs were gigantic talus slopes. Far above them, stray boulders were balanced precariously along the sides of mountains that appeared to be almost perpendicular. They looked as though the slightest nudge would have sent them hurtling down into the icy green water of the fjord, as indeed it would have. For the surfaces of the rocks are constantly being broken up by frost; the smaller particles are then washed down the slopes by rain and melt-water, while the harder lumps remain perched on the eroded surface.

Judy Point, in Victoria Bay, is a long, rocky projection sticking out from the north shore, and forming a well-protected inner harbour. The bits of Frobisher's coal that Charles Francis Hall had discovered 100 years ago were still clearly visible on the surface. They were

scattered across three or four small level spots between the rock outcrops, the only places there where a tent could be pitched. It still
seems strange to me that Hall could find traces of Frobisher's smaller
camps still visible after the passage of 300 years, and that I could
find them just as easily after another 100 years. The scattering of coal,
like similar ones on Kodlunarn Island and Newland Island, probably
marked one of the places where Frobisher's goldfiners had set up their
furnaces or retorts.

We returned to camp about 1:00 p.m., had a quick lunch, then
loaded the entire crew aboard the long-liner for an examination of
Newland and Willows islands. I did not bother searching for the coal
deposit that Hall reported finding on Newland Island, because I was
too pressed for time. We simply examined the shoreline through binoculars, looking for signs of quarrying or mining. So far, I had found
one mine and three quarries in Countess of Warwick Sound, apart
from those on Kodlunarn Island. In addition, Dave had reported
finding another quarry in Napoleon Bay the previous evening, just a
short distance north of our camp. It was quite clear, by that time, that
Frobisher's men had attacked every visible outcrop of red rock in
the immediate vicinity. They had concentrated, however, on those
that looked richest to them. And I could see why Frobisher and his
men believed that the country was incredibly rich in minerals. For
many of the rock outcrops sparkled on a sunny day like jewels, with
the glitter of feldspar, quartz, quartzite, and mica. In the evening we
took a canoe into Diana Bay, to examine and photograph a mine that
we had located just around the corner from our camp. I also wanted to
photograph Christy Creek, a frivolous little stream at the bottom of
the bay that sweeps under a bridge of snow in the valley, and then
bounces down a series of boulder-strewn shelves to the sea.

The next day, August 17, we returned to Kodlunarn Island for some
final photography and measurements. Frobisher's house, as near as
we could determine, had inside measurements of 8½ by 11 feet. The
foundation was of rubble masonry, held together with soft, crumbly
mortar. Roughly accurate measurements were obtained for the thick-
ness of the east and north walls. These measurements were 1½ feet
and 2 feet respectively.

The pit that Charles Francis Hall referred to as a "mine or
reservoir" was definitely a mine or quarry. Frobisher, as we know from
his journal, used water from a pond on the island, and had no need
of a reservoir. Had he needed water, he could have sent his men to
fetch it from any number of streams entering the sound. This mine,

however, was different from all of the other mining operations that we saw, in that it was apparently dug through very broken-up and friable material. All of the other mining or quarrying operations were done by picking, sledging, or hand-spiking off chunks of the laminated but quite solid rock.

There is a rock cairn just north of Frobisher's house, which bears an inscription engraved on a thin plaque of either brass or copper. The plaque is wired on to the cairn and reads:

THIS CAIRN WAS ERECTED
IN MEMORY OF
SIR MARTIN FROBISHER
as a centennial project by

LT. A. BROCKLEY

DR. R. WEST

MR. V. BROCKLEY

FROBISHER BAY 11.7.66.

Along the east end of Kodlunarn Island is a poorly defined ridge having a knoll at each end, more or less. On the east side of the southern knoll is the outline of what was probably a blacksmith shop. The structure measures 25 by 22 feet, with the long axis running north and south. From the south wall of the building to the edge of the eroded bank in the cove north of Best's Bulwark is 67 feet. All that remains of the house is the low ridges of earth that mark the location

Frobisher's house on Kodlunarn Island

of three of the walls. The east wall was apparently snug up against the rock base of the knoll. There is an obvious concentration of stones on the floor of the building, but they form no discernible pattern. Both brick fragments and small nut-sized lumps of coal could be seen peeking through the moss. I did not wish to disturb the structure, as it was too late in the season to excavate it properly and any exploratory work that we might do could very well lead the curious to do some digging of their own. A small test pit was dug near the edge of the cove, however, and showed that the thin lens of coal that we first noted along the eroded bank was probably washed down the slope from some spot higher up. At the top of the slope is the structure that I have tentatively named "the blacksmith shop".

In the afternoon, we took the long-liner into Napoleon and Lincoln bays for a final examination of the rock formations, and to examine a quarry that Dave had found just around the corner from Seagull Rock, a vertical cliff just east of our camp. Behind the ridge at the north of our camp was a beautiful alpine meadow studded with rocks and sloping gently down to the shores of Napoleon Bay. At the foot of the valley was an old Eskimo encampment, apparently a summer camp only, as I did not see any winter houses. The tent-rings and sleeping-platforms were very neatly made, however, suggesting a degree of permanence. A small fragment of heavily oxidized European copper, together with a couple of fragments of what appeared to be Frobisher's coal, suggested that this might be one of the camps that was inhabited when Frobisher appeared in the sound.

Between the old Eskimo camp and Seagull Rock we found a small quarry where Frobisher's men had battered off chunks of a pegmatite dike. We photographed the quarry but did not bother collecting any rock samples, as we already had adequate specimens of everything that Frobisher was mining and quarrying in the sound.

One problem had still not been solved to my satisfaction: how to distinguish with reasonable certainty between the quarrying activities of Frobisher's miners and the breaking up of the rocks through natural agencies. With the larger mines and quarries there was no problem. What was bothering me was the smaller quarries. How was I to know that these—or some of them, perhaps—were not due to natural agencies? They might, for example, be the results of differential weathering patterns. I therefore decided to explore Napoleon Bay and Lincoln Bay a second time to see if natural agencies attacked the red stone that Frobisher had been mining in Countess of Warwick Sound differently from the other rock formations in the area.

View from Seagull Rock

As we cruised about, I swept the shore with field-glasses to see whether the red outcrops did, in fact, occur throughout the region, or whether they were limited to Countess of Warwick Sound; and if they did occur, whether they were weathered in some manner that I might confuse with quarrying. The results of my examination were quite conclusive. First, the outcrops of red rock that were so battered in the sound did occur throughout the area. Second, any differential weathering was so slight that it was not visible from even a short distance away. I concluded, therefore, that all those places in the sound that looked like quarries actually were quarries, rather than the results of ice-battering, or of frost or wave action.

By that time, everyone was exhausted, and quite apprehensive about the weather, as I was myself, and so we agreed that we would break camp on August 18 if at all possible. We were up early that morning, and after breakfast we repacked some of the groceries and rolled up our personal gear and sleeping bags. The weather was extremely unsettled, with wide patches of warm blue sky, and other patches that threatened to inundate us at any moment. The wind was equally unsettled, blowing, it seemed, from several different directions at once. Then, about 8:30, Joanasee arrived with the long-liner and announced that the weather was fine for travelling. We immediately struck all the tents, rolled them up, carried everything to the beach, and started ferrying it out to the vessel in the two canoes. I stayed on shore to the end, then after a final look around, climbed rather sadly into one of the boats.

Aboard the big boat, I counted nine Eskimo of assorted ages. With the eight members of my own party, that made a total complement of seventeen people aboard a forty-four-foot work-boat that was designed to provide cramped quarters for three. As we left the anchorage beside Chambers Reef I remained on deck taking my last look at the bay, while Mosesee headed south around Kodlunarn Island. Then, as the island dropped astern, a gentle rain started to fall, gradually washing out the Harris Highlands to the east. And so we passed through the narrow strait between Cape Sarah and Newland Island and headed northwest for the town of Frobisher Bay.

As soon as we had rounded Cape Sarah and could no longer see Countess of Warwick Sound, everyone started to search for a comfortable spot to settle into. And of course there were not nearly enough spots to go around. About five of us managed to wedge ourselves into the forecastle, while the remainder were forced to stand on deck. From time to time we would change places, but mostly we just suffered in silence while the weather gradually deteriorated. The one saving grace was Joanasee's eight-year-old son, Noah. He was a thoroughly delightful lad, and one of infinite flexibility. No matter how crowded a bunk might be, Noah would always be able to find some corner that he could wedge himself into. He was obviously very proud of being down the bay with the men. At the same time he was young enough to be able to crawl into the forecastle without any loss of status, and he spent hours there, talking, sleeping, and eating pilot biscuits. His presence was the one thing that could take our minds off the uncomfortable roll of the vessel and the dismal situation in which we found ourselves.

When we were planning the return trip, we had agreed that we would not keep travelling all night as we had when we came down the bay. To spend a solid eighteen- to twenty-hour stretch in that tiny cramped vessel was just too exhausting, and so it was agreed that we would go about half way up the bay, and then go ashore for the night. By mid-afternoon, however, when Joanasee asked me what time I wanted to set up camp, I had changed my mind. The thought of dragging all that wet gear ashore in the rain suddenly seemed pointless. We might just as well stay where we were and continue to put up with miseries to which we were thoroughly habituated by that time. The occasional flake of wet, soggy snow tended to reinforce my decision. When I raised the matter with the crew, they were of the same opinion. So the decision was made: we would keep running all night, with the expectation of being put ashore at Frobisher Bay by ten or eleven o'clock the next morning.

A short while later, I was sitting in the forecastle having a cup of tea and a pilot biscuit with Noah when the vessel suddenly lurched violently to port. I climbed out on deck to see what was happening and noticed that the vessel was almost stopped. I could see no reason for stopping—certainly we had not run into anything—and there was no apparent reason for the sudden change of course. The Eskimo were scurrying about, but they seemed perfectly calm, and I concluded that there was probably nothing to worry about. I returned to my tea, and in a few minutes the vessel was again under way. When Noah entered the forecastle a little later, I asked him what had happened, but he had seen nothing and had not bothered to ask. We had just stopped speculating on what might have happened, when the vessel again gave a sudden lurch to port. This time when I crawled out on deck I sought out Joanesee to see what was happening, and learned that the steering cable had parted. No one seemed greatly concerned, although I admit to a mild anxiety when I saw one of the crew heading for the engine room with a roll of scotch tape. Whatever he did must have worked, however, for we were soon back on course.

But it turned out that the repairs were only temporary, for Joanasee told me that we would have to stop for the night and complete the repairs in the morning. In addition, the weather had deteriorated to the point where it was unwise to continue. Mosesee, by that time, had worked the vessel into the centre of a clutch of small islands just off Opera Glass Cape, where we dropped anchor. As usual, the Eskimo had figured out what should be done before they approached me. When they did approach me it was with the following proposition, which we immediately put into effect. The three women were to spend the night in the forecastle, Frank and I were to sleep in the hold, and one of the crew was to sleep in the wheelhouse. The rest of the party—nine men and two boys—wedged themselves, their sleeping bags, and a ten-by-twelve-foot tent into one of the canoes and went ashore for the night. Although I was rather cramped in the tiny bunk in the hold, I did get a few hours' sleep. At one point, I was awakened by a noise that I had trouble identifying, until I realized that it was Frank talking Eskimo in his sleep. He was muttering something about a caribou— one of the few words that I recognize in his language—and was probably stalking it across one of the rock-strewn mountains that he was so fond of climbing. Being older and less nimble than Frank, I left him to his hunting, rolled over, and went back to sleep. When I woke up an hour or so later, the hunt was over and must have been successful, for Frank was quietly sleeping.

The next morning, August 19, while the rest of us had an early breakfast, two or three of the men worked on the steering cable. They soon had it working to their satisfaction, and manoeuvred the vessel out of the small nest of islands in which we had spent the night. Again, the day was cold and raw, with a brisk wind out of the southeast. The following seas were becoming uncomfortably high, when the steering cable broke for the third time. We were bounced around rather violently as the vessel fell off into one of the troughs, but she settled down to a steady roll as soon as the clutch was disengaged. This time the crew made no attempt to repair the cable but rigged a tiller for the rest of the homeward voyage.

In the late afternoon, when we arrived at Frobisher Bay, I picked up the binoculars to examine two other long-liners that were anchored there. Like our own vessel, neither of them had a name. As we headed ashore in the canoe, I glanced back for a final look at our own nameless craft, and at her high, graceful bows where I would have been tempted to paint the name "Polaris". And then it struck me that her anonymity was quite fitting, for the land we were exploring was still called "Meta Incognita".

Appendix

Index

Appendix

The Frobisher Minerals

The rocks collected from Martin Frobisher's mines in Countess of Warwick Sound, Frobisher Bay, Baffin Island, were submitted for analysis to Dr. Sydney B. Lumbers, Curator of the Department of Geology, the Royal Ontario Museum. Dr. Lumbers very kindly examined the collection, which consists of ninety-nine different rock specimens. After a detailed visual inspection, he selected sixteen specimens for petrographic examination. Following his study, Dr. Lumbers reported as follows:

> Most of the rocks from the Frobisher workings are derived from sandstones, but these rocks were altered by heat and pressure (regionally metamorphosed) to such an extent that most primary sedimentary features except relic bedding were either destroyed or obscured. This metamorphism presents problems in classifying the rocks according to their primary characteristics. For example, original rock fragments may have been destroyed by the metamorphism, and original clay minerals were recrystallized into other mineral species. If one assumes that most of the mica (biotite + muscovite) present in the rocks is derived from clay minerals (as is commonly the case), then most of the metasandstones represent arkosic sandstones containing thin beds of shale or mudstone. Some of the shaley rocks were calcareous, and these produced the calc-silicate gneisses. A few of the quartz-rich metasandstones (spec. 11 & 15) were probably derived from subarkose.

> Although sequences of arkosic sandstones with intercalated shales are typically deposited in shallow water above wave-base, much more geological data would be needed to speculate on details of the original depositional environment of this rock sequence.

> Note that opaque metallic minerals are present in all of the rocks examined. Such minerals are normally found in rocks of this type and in the quantities present. There is no suggestion of gold mineralization, or of any abnormal concentration of metallic minerals of any composition in the rocks examined.

Although our investigation into the nature of the Frobisher minerals was limited to Countess of Warwick Sound, we may safely accept the specimens which we collected there as typifying the Frobisher minerals

Rocks from **Frobisher's** mines in Countess of Warwick Sound

generally. For we know from the various journals of the Frobisher voyages that the rocks they were collecting throughout the area consisted mainly of a "black ore" which Dr. Lumbers has now identified as calc-silicate gneiss, and a "red ore" which he has identified as a metasandstone. Frobisher's men would also have picked up stray bits of quartz, feldspar, mica, and similar minerals, but these were incidental. We know, further, that the flecks of "gold" which glistened in the sands of so many beaches in the area were actually flecks of biotite mica.

And now, finally, Canada's first gold-rush is over. The fever has subsided, and the workings are abandoned once more. After the passage of 400 years there is really nothing else to say except, perhaps, to warn the unwary, as Frobisher himself was warned so many years ago, that "all is not gold that shineth".

Index

Achilles, 21
Adventurers to the Northwest for
 the Discovery of a Northwest
 Passage, 10
Aegean Sea, 24
Africa, 4, 6, 22, 23, 24
Agnello, John Baptista, 121
Aid, xi, 45, 46, 49, 53, 55, 57, 58,
 59, 77, 93, 106, 110
Air Canada, 126
Alexander the Great, 21, 22, 23
Alexandria, 34 fn.
Altars of Alexander, 23
America, 24, 26, 30, 33, 40, 49,
 54, 63, 89
Anne Frances, 77, 79, 84, 86, 87,
 90, 93, 97, 98, 99, 101, 102,
 103, 104, 106, 107, 110, 111,
 112
Apex, 126
Arabia, 33
Argonaut Press, xi
Aristotle, 19
Armenia, 22
Armshaw, William, 46
Asia, 22, 23, 24, 28, 40
Astrakhan, 30
Atlantic Ocean, 8, 24, 26, 69

Baccalaos, 29
Baffin Island, xi, 122, 124, 133,
 135, 157
Barbary, 22
Bay of Mexico, 80
Bay of St. Nicholas, 30
Bear, 77, 79
Beare, James, 46, 86
Beare's Sound, 14, 56, 107, 108,
 110, 111, 112
Benin, 4, 30, 32
Best, George, xi, xii, 15, 17, 45,
 55, 76, 77, 95, 104, 105, 106,
 107, 119

Best's Blessing, 14, 103
Best's Bulwark, 66, 133, 138, 143,
 144, 148
Bilbill, 30
Black Sea, 24
Blackwall, 38, 45, 46
Bloody Point, 59
Bona Confidentia, 5
Bona Esperanza, 5
Bond, William, 7
Borough, Stephen, 6, 7, 29 fn.
Borough, William, 29 fn.
Brackenburye, Frauncis, 46
Brazil, 3, 30
Bristol, 10, 30, 72, 79
Brockley, Lt. A., 148
Brockley, V., 148
Burde, William, 7

Cabot, Sebastian, 6, 7, 30
Canada, xi, 116
Canary Islands, 3, 4
Cape Clear, 79
Cape de las Palmas, 32
Cape Dorset, 137
Cape of Good Hope, 24, 26, 37, 80
Cape Sarah, 130, 151
Carew, Henry, 45, 77, 95, 111
Caspian Sea, 30
Catchoe, 66, 68
Cathay, 14, 26, 29, 30, 37, 41, 42,
 49, 75, 76, 87, 96, 108
Chamberlain, Tho., 46
Chambers, John, 126, 127
Chambers Reef, 151
Chancellor, Richard, 5, 25
Charing, Mrs. Jean, xii
Charing Cross, 81
China, 49
Christopher Hall Island, 138
Christy Creek, 147
Cicero, 19
Cobourg, 126

Coke, Sir Edward, vi
Collinson, R., xi
Columbus, Christopher, 3
Company of Cathai, 10
Company of Merchants Adventurers of England for the Discovery of Lands, Territories, Isles, Dominions, and Seigniories unknown, 6
Conger, Nicholas, 52
Cornwall, 37, 71
Countess of Sussex Mine, 14, 106, 110
Countess of Warwick Island, 10, 14, 15, 63, 66, 67, 96, 97, 107
Countess of Warwick Sound, xi, 14, 58, 62, 91, 93, 95, 101, 105, 106, 107, 108, 110, 122, 123, 124, 126, 130, 137, 143, 147, 149, 151, 157
Courtney, Capt., 77
Coutinho, Miss Margaret, xii
Cox, Richard, 46, 53, 99
Coxe, Mr., 102

Daniels, Miss Peta, xii
Dartford, 10
Dartford Creek, 109
Davis Strait, 123, 124, 138, 141
Dawson, Irene, 126
Demosthenes, 19
Denmark, 34
Dennis, 77, 79, 82, 88
Devonshire, 37
Diana Bay, 147
Don River, 24 fn.
Downie, Mrs. Helen, xi
Dudley, Ambrose, Earl of Warwick, 7, 38, 42, 50
Dudley, John, Duke of Northumberland, 7
Dudley, Robert, Earl of Leicester, 7
Dvina River, 5, 29 fn., 30
Dyer, Andrew, 46, 53
Dyer's Passage, 14

East Indies, 26, 33, 49
Eden, Richard, 4
Edinburgh, 47
Edward Bonaventure, 5, 6, 29 fn.
Elizabeth I, 3, 10
Emanuel of Bridgewater, 77, 79, 91, 91 fn., 110, 111, 112
Emanuel of Exeter, 77, 79, 91 fn.
England, 3, 6, 7, 8, 24, 26, 28, 29, 30, 32, 33, 34, 35, 36, 38, 40, 41, 46, 47, 48, 49, 55, 76, 77, 79, 95, 104, 110, 112, 114, 115, 117, 121
Eoum Sea, 23
Essex, 42, 46
Europe, 3, 6, 19, 22, 23, 24, 28, 48

Fenton, Edward, 14, 46, 55, 67, 76, 77, 82, 93, 94, 95, 98, 107
Fenton's Fortune, 14, 95
Filpot, Capt., 76, 77
Findlay, David, xii
Florence, 35
Forder, Francis, 45
Fortunate Islands, 25
Frances of Foy, 77, 79, 84, 91
Frank, 127, 153
Friesland, 38, 48, 49, 79, 109, 112
Frobisher Bay, 122, 124, 126, 127, 128, 131, 137, 142, 143, 151, 152, 153, 157
Frobisher Inn, 124
Frobisher, Martin, xi, 7, 8, 10, 14, 15, 22, 23, 26, 29, 36, 37, 38, 41, 42, 45, 66, 75, 76, 77, 79, 87 fn., 96, 97, 104, 108, 110, 113, 121, 122, 132, 133, 135, 138, 147, 148, 149, 157, 158
Frobisher Straits, 24, 26, 40, 49, 81, 84, 86, 88, 89, 91, 112, 113, 122
Frozen Sea, 24, 81

Gabriel, 8, 14, 38, 45, 46, 49, 55, 70, 72, 77, 79, 84, 89, 91, 93, 97, 111

Gabriel Island, 105, 130
Ganges, 23
Gemma Frisius, 34
Genoa, Antonius, 48
Genoa, Nicholaus, 48
Germany, 28
Ghana, 4
Gilbert, Sir Humphrey, 5, 6
Gothland, 35
Gravesend, 46
Gray, John, 104
Greece, 22
Greenland, 25, 38 fn., 77, 81, 89
Gresham, Sir Thomas, 7
Grinnell Glacier, 123, 124, 128
Guinea, 4, 7, 30, 32
Gulf of Mexico, 88

Hakluyt Society, xi, 5
Hall, Charles Francis, 122, 132, 133, 134, 137, 140, 146, 147
Hall, Christopher, 46, 49, 78, 86, 87, 95
Hall's Island, 49, 50, 87 fn., 108, 121
Hall's Land, 49, 50
Hall's Sound, 50
Hamilton, 126
Harris Highlands, 124, 141, 151
Harvie, Capt., 45, 77
Harwich, 46, 77, 79
Hatton's Headland, 90, 91, 92, 103, 104, 106
Hawkins, William, 3, 4
Hawkins, Sir John, 3
Hebrides, 24
Henry VII, 30
Henry VIII, 3, 28
Hercules, 22
Holywood, John, 34 fn.
Hopewell, 79, 111
Hosek, Mrs. Georgina, xii
Hudson Strait, 87 fn., 122, 126

Iceland, 23, 24, 47, 88
Icy Sea, 50
India, 22, 29, 33

Ireland, 48, 79, 80, 88
Irene Lake, 135
Isle of St. Thomas, 32
Isle of Wight, 50
Isles of Orcades, 47
Ivan IV, Czar, 5

Jackman, Charles, 46, 53, 59, 95
Jackman Sound, 54, 55, 57, 58, 62
James Bay, 126
Jenkinson, Anthony, 30
Joanasee, 127, 134, 135, 137, 142, 151, 152, 153
Judith, 14, 77, 79, 82, 110
Judy Point, 146
Julius Caesar, 21

Keeble, K. C., xii
Kegor, 5
Kendall, Capt., 77
Kenyon, Diane, 126
Kholmogory, 5
King, Dr. Henry B., xii
Kinnersley, Capt., 77
Kirkwall, 47 fn.
Kodlunarn Island, 122, 130, 132, 134, 135, 137, 138, 141, 147, 148, 151
Kynersley, Mathew, 45
Kynersley, Robert, 46
Kyrway, 47

La Mina, 4
Lake Harbour, 137
Lakes, John, 99
Land's End, 71
Lapland, 5, 24, 25, 30, 31 fn.
Lee, John, 45
Lee, Michael, xii, 126, 127, 130
Leicester Point, 99
Leicester's Island, 56
Levant Company, 10
Lightwood, Dave, 126, 128, 147, 149
Lincoln Bay, 135, 141, 149
Lion, 4

Lofoten Islands, 5
Lok, Michael, 7, 8, 10, 110, 121, 122
London Bridge, 86
London, England, xi, 5, 10, 41, 121
London, Ontario, 126
Louvain, 34 fn.
Lumbers, Dr. Sydney B., xii, 157, 158
Lundy, 71
Lycurgus, 19
Lyons, Abraham, 46

Macedonia, 22
Madeira, 4
Magellan, 40
Mare Congelatum, 24
Mare de Sur, 49
Mare Eoum, 24
Mare Glaciale, 49, 50
Mare Pacificum, 49
Marsh, Judy, 126, 141
McKenzie, Bill, 126
Mediterranean Sea, 24
Mercator, 24
Meta Incognita, 14, 37, 58, 75, 76, 80, 81, 82, 94, 96, 109, 110, 113, 114, 117, 123, 154
Michael, 8, 14, 38, 45, 46, 47, 49, 55, 56, 58, 59, 70, 72, 77, 79, 82, 93, 111
Milford Haven, 71, 72
Mistaken Straits, 87, 87 fn., 88, 89, 90, 91, 98, 99, 108, 113
Molucca, 33
Montreal, 122, 126
Moon, 77, 79, 84, 93, 97, 98, 99, 102, 103, 104
Moosonee, 126
Morbus Gallicus, 117
Morocco, 32, 33
Moscow, 5, 113, 114
Mosesee, 127, 128, 130, 134, 151, 153
Mount Oxford, 97, 98
Mount Warwick, 50, 51, 86, 138
Mountains of the Moon, 23

Moyles, Capt., 77
Muscovy, 14, 24, 26, 28, 29, 30, 31, 34
Muscovy Company, 7, 10, 25 fn., 29 fn., 30 fn.
Muskoka, 137

Naples, 35
Napoleon Bay, 134, 135, 147, 149
Native Point, 134, 141, 144
Newfoundland, 29 fn., 49, 63
Newland Island, 130, 147, 151
Newton, Capt., 77
Nile River, 23
Noah, 152
Nordair, 126
North Foreland, 49, 50, 84, 87 fn.
North Sea, 24, 112
Norway, 5, 24, 25, 30, 80, 88

Ob River, 7, 26, 29
Opera Glass Cape, 153
Ophir, 20
Orcades, 46
Orkney Islands, 23, 24, 28, 46, 47, 70
Ortelius, 24

Pacific Ocean, 26
Padstowe Road, 71
Pangnirtung, 137
Paul of Plymouth, 3
Persia, 22, 30
Peta Point, 135
Philpot, Richard, 45, 95
Pillars of Hercules, 22
Pilot, Robert, xii
Pinteado, Anthonie Anes, 4
Plymouth, 4
Poland, 28
Pond Inlet, 126
Pootaliq, 127
Pope Alexander VI, 3
Pope Sixtus IV, 3
Portugal, 3, 4
Postel, Guillaume, 25